Tips

▸ Help your child focus on the tasks by minimizing distractions such as television.

▸ Explain directions before your child begins a new type of activity.

▸ Check your child's work and help correct errors. Praise a job well done!

▸ Encourage your child to talk about the work. For example, what did he or she like or not like about the task?

Supplies

▸ crayons or colored pencils

▸ marking pens

▸ pencil

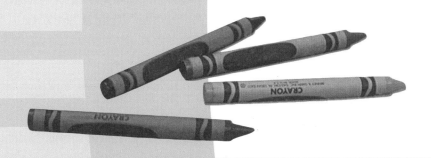

Table of Contents

Puzzling Pictures
Spelling................4

It Happened to Me
Creative Writing................5

Ollie and the Yarn
Measurement................6

Hey Diddle Riddle!
Context Clues................7

A Lunchroom Mess
Spelling................8

The Circle-T Ranch
Shapes................9

Secret Agent Elephant Gray
Word Families................10

Flower Power!
Short and Long Vowels................11

Less Mess Is Best
Subtraction................12

Pig Scramble!
Spelling................13

Make the Connection
Alphabetical Order................14

Pizza Party
Fractions................15

Step on Down!
Spelling................16

Opposites
Antonyms................17

Just for Mom
Odd and Even Numbers................18

Brand New Nursery Rhymes
Creative Thinking................19

Twelve Months of Missing Vowels
Spelling................20

Leon's Lemonade Stand
Money................21

Choo-choo! Choo-choo!
Sound Words................22

Tock! Tick! The Clock Is Sick!
Word Families................23

Diamond Drop
Number Order................24

Make It Rhyme
Word Family................25

What's in the Box?
Compound Words................26

Count the Cards
Place Value................27

What's Here?
Long and Short Vowels................28

Happy Endings
Plurals................29

T-Shirt Trouble
Patterns................30

Pow! Bang! Kerplop!
Sound Words................31

We'll Go Fishing
Contractions................32

Dot 2 Dot
Counting by 2s................33

What Animal Are You Like?
Creative Writing................34

Nine Fine Fill-ins
Word Families................35

A Penny Saved
Place Value................36

The Spelling Well
Spelling................37

Simple Similes
Similes................38

In the Clock Shop
Telling Time................39

You Say Good-bye; I Say Hello
Antonyms................40

Short and Sweet
Abbreviations................41

Ziggy's Zoo!
Reading a Graph................42

Seasons and Senses
Sensory Details................43

Drew's Dream
/dr/ Blend................44

Riddle Time
Subtraction Facts................45

Cat-Sitter's Questionnaire
Writing................46

Tongue Twisters
Sentence Order................47

Strike Out the Numbers!
Number Patterns................48

Race for the Cheese
Spelling................49

Farmer Sam's BIG Trouble
Word Families................50

I Love Cookies!
Money................51

Terrific Twos
Compound Words................52

Can a Fly Fly in a Can?
Nouns and Verbs................53

Secret Message
Column Addition................54

Shhhhhh! She's Sleeping!
/sh/, /sk/, and /sl/ Blends................55

Use Your Senses!
Creative Writing................56

Round and Round We Go
Count by 5s................57

Fun in the Sun
Vocabulary................58

My Best Friends
Descriptive Writing................59

What Time Is It?
Time................60

It's a Snap!
Long and Short a................61

Every Body
Vocabulary................62

Marble Madness
Problem Solving................63

"A" or "An" Tells What I Am
a or an................64

Pick a Pair
Homophones................65

At the Pet Store
Problem Solving................66

Here Kitty, Kitty, Kitty!
Visual Discrimination................67

Aunt Abby's Attic Alphabet
Creative Thinking....................68

Pick a Lunch!
Graphs 69

Tame Game
Rhyming 70

My Very Own Kingdom
Creative Thinking................... 71

Button, Button, Who Has a Button?
Fractions................................72

Puzzling Palindromes
Palindromes 73

Do You Want a Bat or a Bat?
Homophones 74

Count the Shapes
Geometric Shapes 75

Match the Action
Synonyms 76

I Won't Do It!
Contractions...........................77

Yard Sale Today!
Addition..................................78

Recipe for a Sandwich
Creative Writing 79

Words on the Move
Verbs 80

Riddle Time
Two-Digit Addition and Subtraction............................. 81

Rhyme Time
Rhyming Words 82

Rainy Day Riddles
Context Clues.........................83

Stick the Stamps
Two-Digit Addition.................84

Strange Soup
Classifying 85

Sally's Spill
Synonyms 86

Busy, Busy Garden
Fractions.................................87

Betsy Bee's Busy Day
Context Clues..........................88

Silly Salad
Word Play 89

Do You Have Change for a V?
Roman Numerals.....................90

String Thing
/str/ Blend 91

Through the Trees
/tr/, /thr/ Blends..................92

Aunt Betsy's Bakery
Subtraction 93

Join the Club
Classifying 94

Dear Diary
Journaling 95

A Word's Worth
Addition...................................96

What Was That?
Punctuation.............................97

How Do They Compare?
Comparisons............................98

Crazy About Crayons
Greater Than, Less Than, Equal To...................................99

First, Next, and Last
Sequencing.............................100

Feeling Tip Top
Word Family 101

Ride the Rainbow
Skip Counting 102

Connect Two!
Compound Words 103

Teeny Tiny Tennis Tournament
Descriptive Writing 104

Down by the Sea
Two-Digit Addition..............105

A Book Collection
Alphabetical Order 106

A Pink Mink?
Rhyming, Word Play.............107

Super Candy Sale!
Problem Solving 108

Thanks a Bunch!
Spelling..................................109

Fun with Fill-ins!
Parts of Speech 110

Carly the Coupon Clipper
Two-Digit Subtraction 111

Prefix Pyramids
Prefixes 112

What Am I?
Syllables 113

Sum Time
Addition Facts.......................114

In the Sea
Visual Discrimination............115

The Birthday Bash
Vocabulary 116

Gumball Game
Two-Digit Addition...............117

To the Finish Line!
Creative Thinking..................118

Dear Grandma
Spelling..................................119

Webster's Super Spider Web
Addition.................................120

Put an End to It!
Suffixes 121

Muggsy's Messy Day
Adjectives 122

Three Little Squids
Multiplication Facts 123

What's Hiding?
Nouns 124

What Makes a Perfect Pet?
Narrative Writing.................125

Big-Time Bowling
Addition.................................126

Buy My Stuff
Persuasive Writing 127

Chicken Little Tries Again
Verbs 128

Which Shelf, Elf?
Ordinal Numbers, Reasoning 129

Answer Key............................130

Puzzling Pictures

Use the pictures and the words in the Word Box to fill in the crossword puzzle.

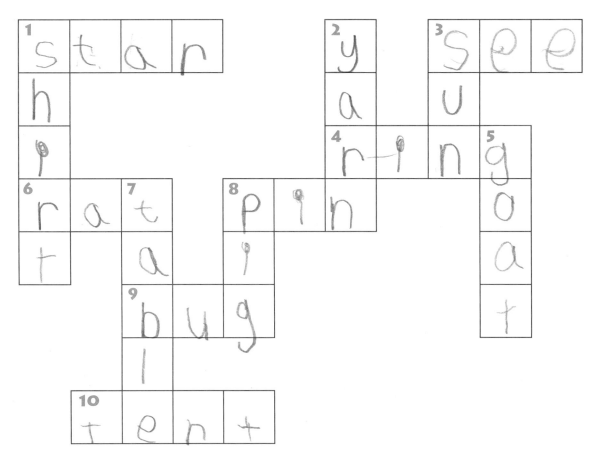

Across

1.

3.

4.

6.

8.

9.

10.

Down

1.

2.

3.

5.

7.

8.

WORD BOX

bug	pig	rat	shirt	table	goat	pin
see	star	tent	sun	yarn	ring	

It Happened to Me

Circle the things you want to have in your story. Then write the rest of the story on the lines below.

One day I decided to go

fishing

skating

shopping

On the way I saw

a kangaroo

some robbers

a bag of money

Now finish your story.

5

Ollie and the Yarn

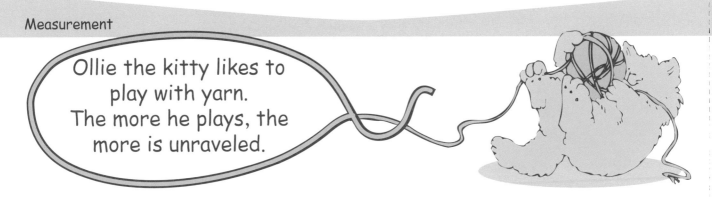

Ollie the kitty likes to play with yarn. The more he plays, the more is unraveled.

Measure each piece of yarn to the closest inch.

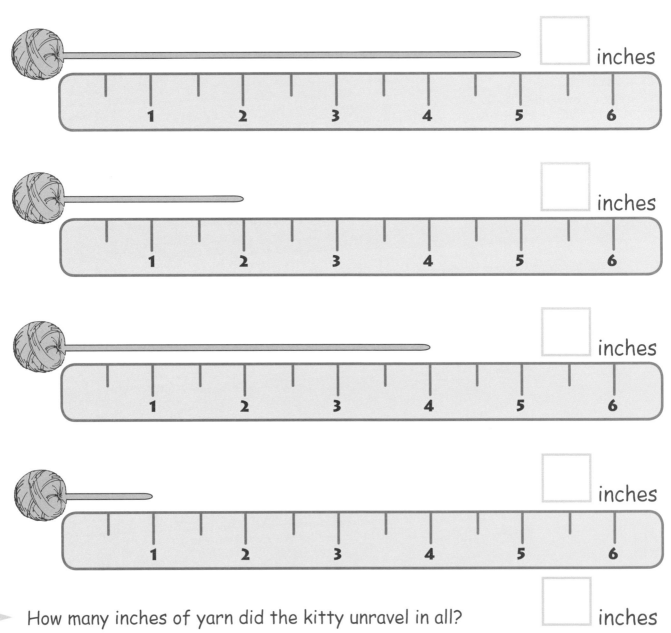

How many inches of yarn did the kitty unravel in all?

Hey Diddle Riddle!

This cat with a fiddle needs help with these riddles. Try to solve the three below.

I am mostly quiet.
But when I'm not, it's time
to talk! Push my buttons! I will
give you a ring!

What am I?

_____

First I am small and flat.
All I need is some air
and I get big and fat.
Tie a knot in my tail or I
will be small and flat again.

What am I?

_____

Hey Diddle Riddle
Write your own riddle!

_____

_____

_____

_____

I fall down, down, down.
I land on your nose
and disappear.
I leave a tiny drop of water.
No one is just like me.

What am I?

_____

I am a _____

A Lunchroom Mess

 Ben and Robert are writing a story about eating lunch. But lots of words are misspelled. Please help clean up this mess of misspelled words.

Circle each word that is spelled wrong. Then write the correct spelling on the lined paper.

It's tyme for lunch! We have fun eeting our lunch with each otehr. Sometimes Ben does magic triks. He can mak my spoon disappear. Can he make it come bak? Of course, he kan. Ben knows I want to eat my soop. I can make hiz milk disappear. I just put in my straw and drinck it all down!

I Can Spell

1.
2.
3.
4.
5.
6.
7.
8.
9.
10.

8

The Circle-T Ranch

Shapes

 Howdy, partner! Welcome to the Circle-T Ranch.

We need your help to round up some shapes for us.
Get out your crayons! Here's what to do:

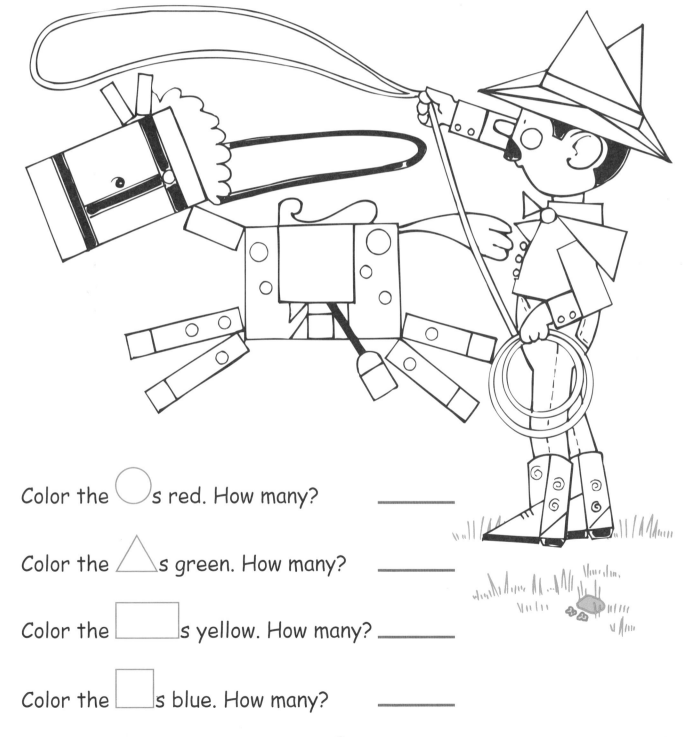

Color the ◯s red. How many? _____

Color the △s green. How many? _____

Color the ▭s yellow. How many? _____

Color the ▢s blue. How many? _____

Secret Agent Elephant Gray

Secret Agent Elephant Gray wants to share his secret code with you. What do you say?

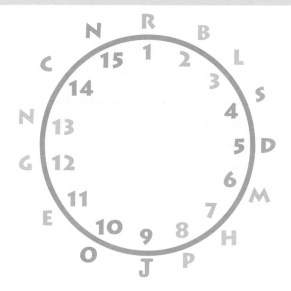

Use the code wheel to find the correct letter for each blank below. Then you can read Secret Agent Gray's secret message!

In two ___ays, bring a bale of ___ay to the ___ ___ayground.
5   7   8   3

___ay it under the tree where the blue ___ay lives.
3   9

I will ___ay you for it on ___ ___ ___ ___ay.
8   6   10   13   5

___ay hello to your friend ___ay. I ___ay buy some
4   1   6

___ay from him ___ ___ ___ ___ ___ay, too.
7   4   10   6   11   5

E. ___ ___ay
12   1

Flower Power!

What a pretty patch of posies!

But they need some color to make them even prettier. You can help!

Read the word in each flower. If the word has a long vowel sound, color that flower purple. If the word has a short vowel sound, color that flower yellow.

11

Less Mess Is Best

Subtraction

Aunt Bess left the kitchen in a mess!
Help her get rid of some items.

Count the number of each item in the picture and then subtract the amount shown below. How many are left?

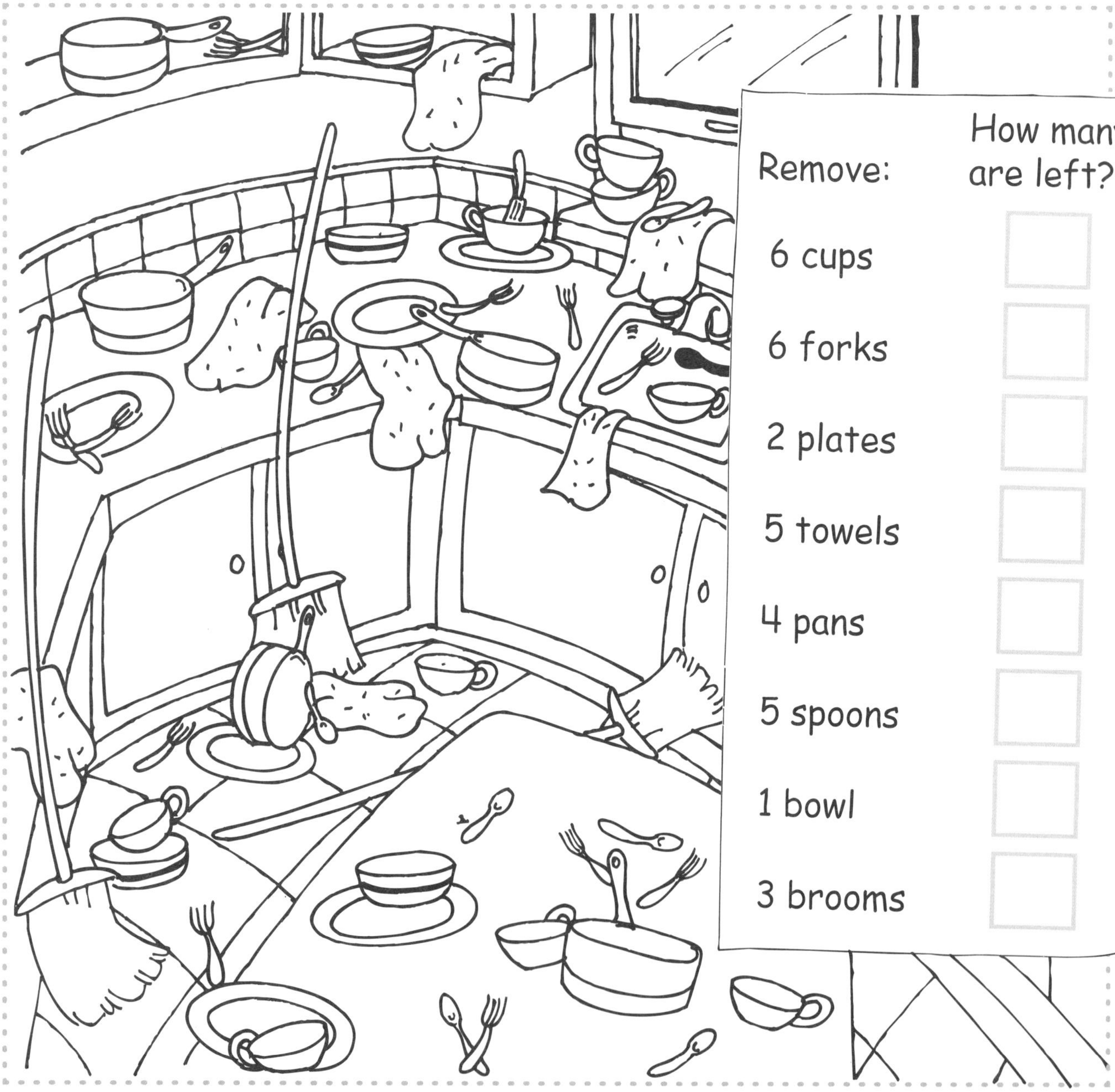

Remove:	How many are left?
6 cups	
6 forks	
2 plates	
5 towels	
4 pans	
5 spoons	
1 bowl	
3 brooms	

Pig Scramble!

What a **crazy** farm!

All of the animals are mixed up.

Unscramble the letters to spell each animal word correctly.

owc   _____ _____ _____

shero   _____ _____ _____ _____ _____

ikhccne _____ _____ _____ _____ _____ _____ _____

pgi   _____ _____ _____

cudk   _____ _____ _____ _____

odg   _____ _____ _____

agot   _____ _____ _____ _____

espeh   _____ _____ _____ _____ _____

erstoro _____ _____ _____ _____ _____ _____

umose   _____ _____ _____ _____ _____

WORD BOX

dog	rooster	duck	horse	mouse
chicken	cow	pig	sheep	goat

Make the Connection

Connect the dots in alphabetical order. Then fill in the blanks below to tell what the picture is.

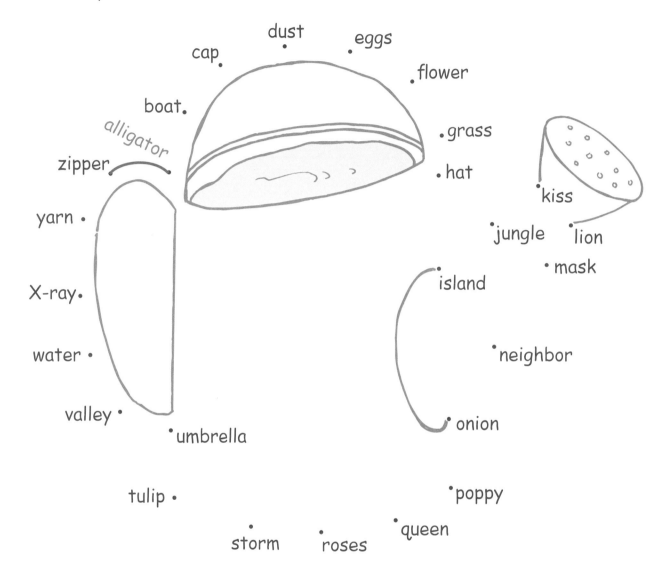

alligator
boat
cap
dust
eggs
flower
grass
hat
island
jungle
kiss
lion
mask
neighbor
onion
poppy
queen
roses
storm
tulip
umbrella
valley
water
X-ray
yarn
zipper

Unscramble these letters:

tewagrni anc

_ _ _ _ _ _ _ _ _

_ _ _

Pizza Party

Pete has lots of pizzas. Some have only cheese and some have pepperoni.

Using the fractions shown below, tell what fraction of each pizza has pepperoni.

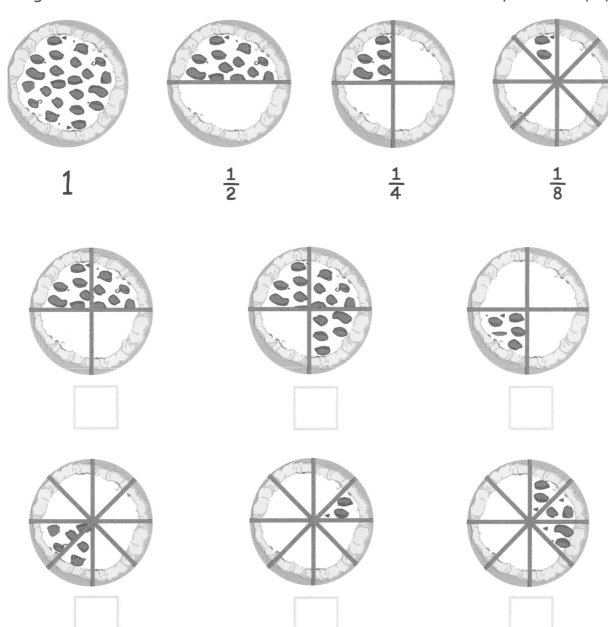

1

$\frac{1}{2}$

$\frac{1}{4}$

$\frac{1}{8}$

Step on Down!

Add letters to each word until you land on the last step. There are lots of answers you can use.

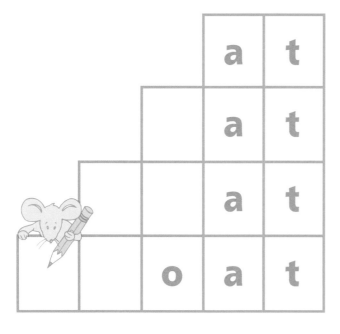

Opposites

> Write the opposite (antonym) of the word given. Use the Word Box to help you.

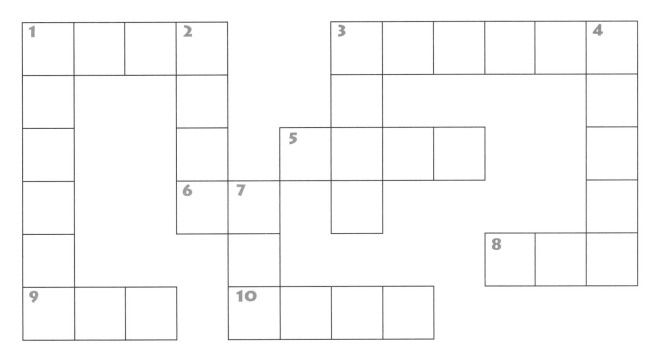

over

Across
1. hot
3. big
5. go
6. yes
8. night
9. wet
10. light

Down
1. opened
2. up
3. early
4. full
7. even

under

WORD BOX

day	dark	cold	odd	stop	empty
late	down	little	dry	no	closed

Just for Mom

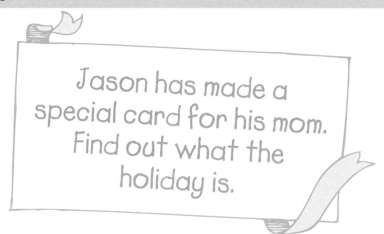

Jason has made a special card for his mom. Find out what the holiday is.

Color even numbers red. Even numbers are those that can be counted by 2.
Color odd numbers green. Odd numbers can **not** be counted by 2.

22	71	3	45	19	27	85	9	46
15	99	10	4	7	8	12	11	35
77	22	36	50	2	14	94	6	97
69	18	20	42	16	28	72	34	55
91	33	66	80	44	26	58	81	79
47	17	87	34	76	62	25	13	31
78	93	61	29	88	73	57	39	80

Which holiday is it?

○ Christmas   ○ Fourth of July

○ Valentine's Day   ○ St. Patrick's Day

Brand New Nursery Rhymes

Add your own words to make these old nursery rhymes new.

Jack and Jill went up the _____

To get a _____ of _____ .

Mary had a little _____ . Its _____ was

_____ as _____ .

Little Boy _____ come blow your _____ ,

The _____ is in the _____ .

Little Miss _____ sat on a _____

Eating her _____ and _____ .

Draw a picture of one of the new rhymes.

Twelve Months of Missing Vowels

Spelling

Someone tried to take the vowels from the months of the year!

Put them back where they belong.

J		N			R	Y		
F		B	R			R	Y	
M		R	C	H				
	P	R		L				
M		Y						
J		N						
J		L	Y					
		G		S	T			
S		P	T		M	B		R
	C	T		B		R		
N		V		M	B		R	
D		C		M	B		R	

Leon's Lemonade Stand

Leon doesn't have a price for his lemonade. He lets the customers pay him whatever they want.

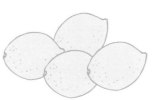

Count the money and write how much each customer gave him.

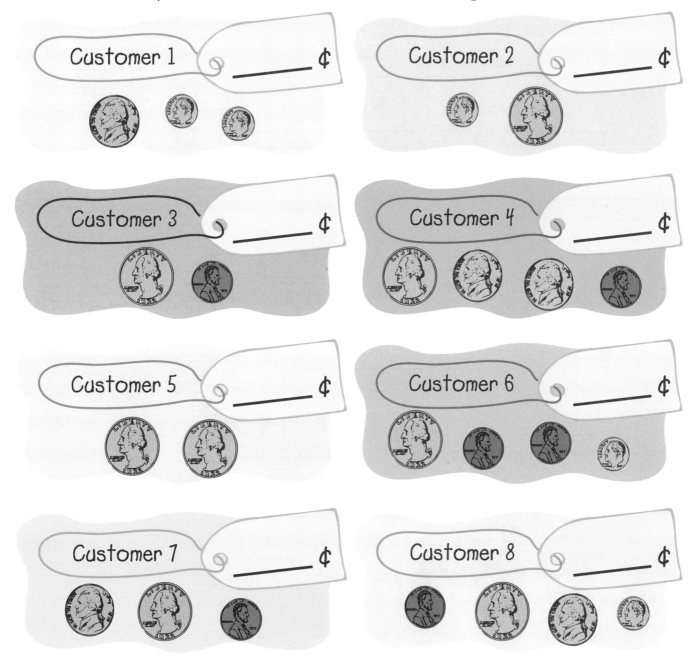

21

Choo-choo! Choo-choo!

Listen to the train. It is carrying lots of sound words (like choo-choo!). Can you complete the words?

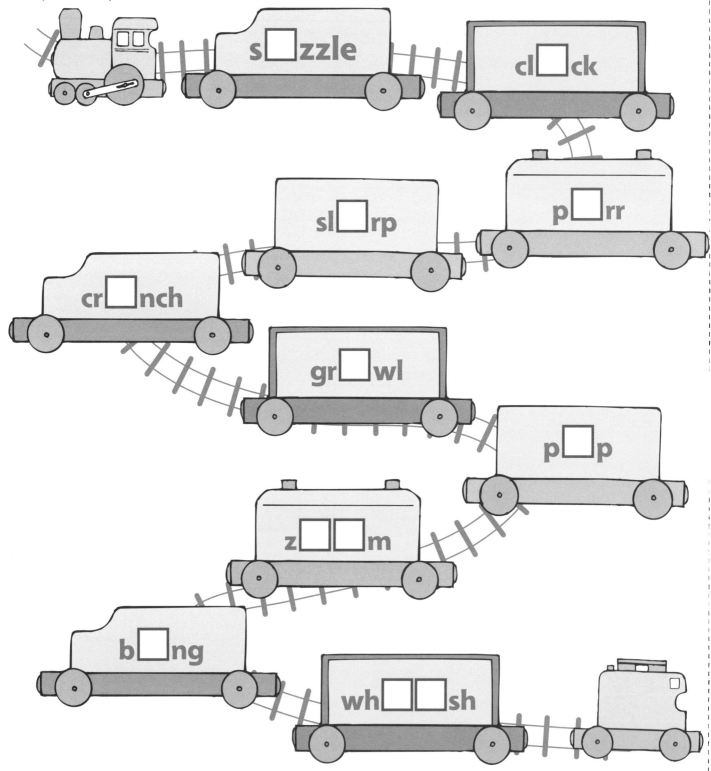

22

Tock! Tick! The Clock Is Sick!

Word Families

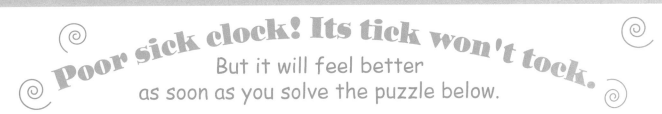

But it will feel better
as soon as you solve the puzzle below.

All of the words belong to the -ick or the -ock families. Fill in the blanks with the correct letters.

dogs do this   ____ ick

thin piece of wood   ____ ____ ick

you do this to a football   ____ ick

a stone   ____ ock

this helps to keep things safe   ____ ock

a bunch of sheep   ____ ____ ock

a baby hen   ____ ____ ick

on your foot   ____ ock

a bug   ____ ick

_____ or treat   ____ ____ ick

Diamond Drop

Darice dropped her diamonds! Help her put them back in order.
Do each row separately. The first one has been done for you.

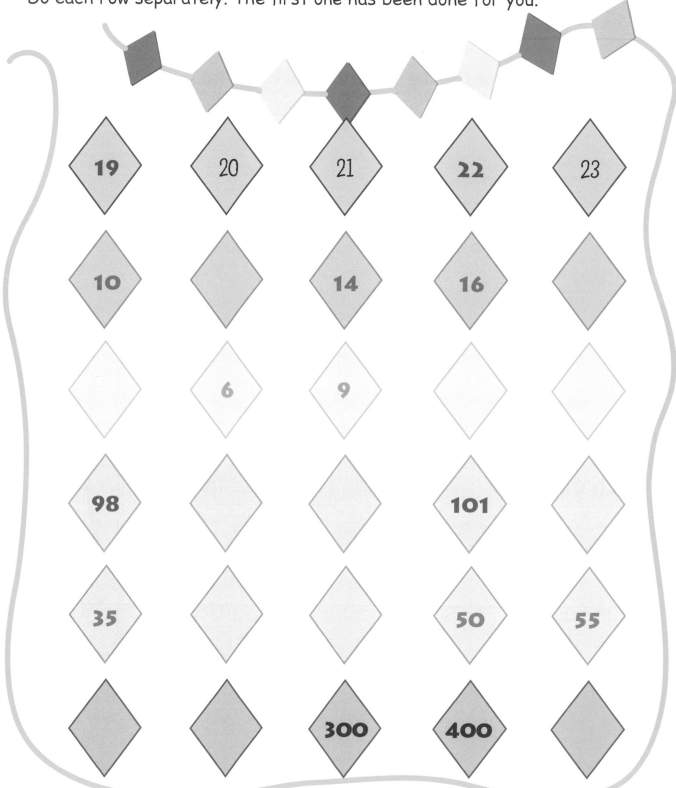

24

Make It Rhyme

Fill in the blanks with -ail words to make a rhyme. Then draw a picture to show what happened.

Fido knocked over the

_____pail_____

When he barked and wagged

his _____tail_____.

She waited and waited for

the _____.

It must have been delivered

by a _____.

Five chicks and Mother

qu_____

Hiked along the forest

_____.

What's in the Box?

Look at all the goodies in the box. Each one is a compound word (a word made of two words put together). Use a word from each list to name each thing in the box.

sea	book
sun	pot
note	stick
air	fly
cow	boy
dragon	plane
tea	flower
candle	shell

_____
_____
_____
_____
_____
_____
_____

Count the Cards

Place Value

Bobby and his friends have a huge baseball card collection. They want to count every single card. Show how many cards each person has.

Bobby 2 hundreds   3 tens   9 ones   _____

Andrew 1 hundred   8 tens   3 ones   _____

Jamie 3 hundreds   0 tens   5 ones   _____

Kelly 2 hundreds   5 tens   1 one   _____

Yoki 3 hundreds   3 tens   0 ones   _____

Write the names in order from the person with the most cards to the one with the fewest cards.

1 _____

2 _____

3 _____

4 _____

5 _____

What's Here?

Find out what is hidden in the picture.

Color the words with short vowels yellow.

Color the words with long vowels blue.

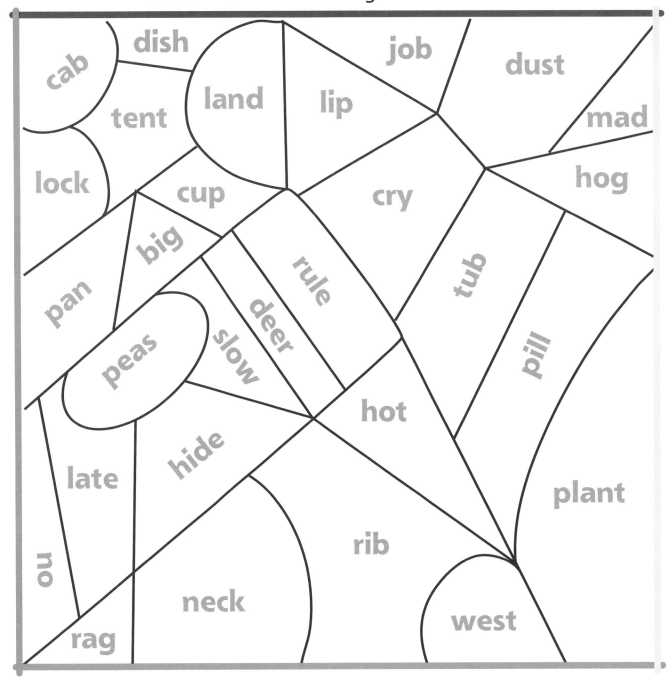

What did you find? _____

Happy Endings

Each of these pictures shows one thing.
But what if there were two?
How would you write the plural word?

Add s to most words to make them plural. But add es to words that end in ch, sh, s, or x.

1 bush

2 _____ _____ _____ _____ _____ _____

1 book

4 _____ _____ _____ _____ _____ _____

1 fox

3 _____ _____ _____ _____ _____ _____

1 bench

2 _____ _____ _____ _____ _____ _____

1 chair

3 _____ _____ _____ _____ _____ _____

1 bus

2 _____ _____ _____ _____ _____ _____

T-Shirt Trouble

Coach Smith has a big problem!
Some of the team T-shirts are missing their numbers. But he has a good idea. He put the shirts in order. Now he can see which numbers are missing.

Can you figure out what number belongs on each shirt?

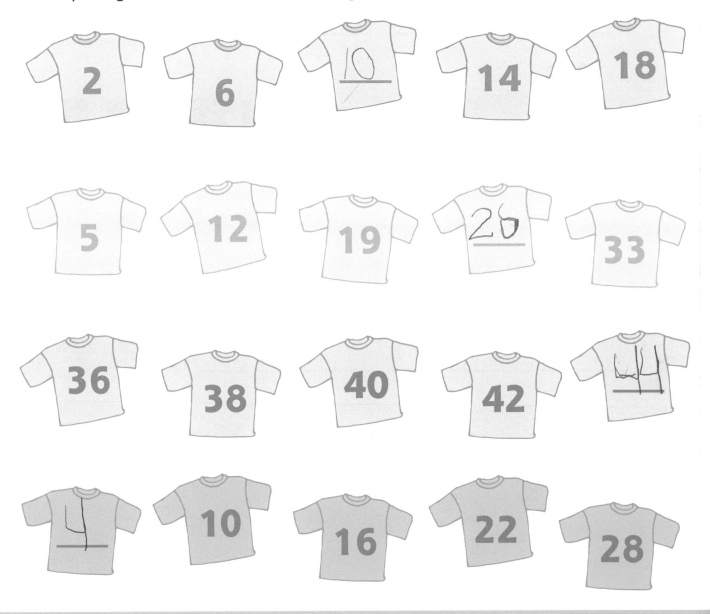

Pow! Bang! Kerplop!

Unscramble these words to see what sound they make. Draw a string from the balloon to the correct sound word below.

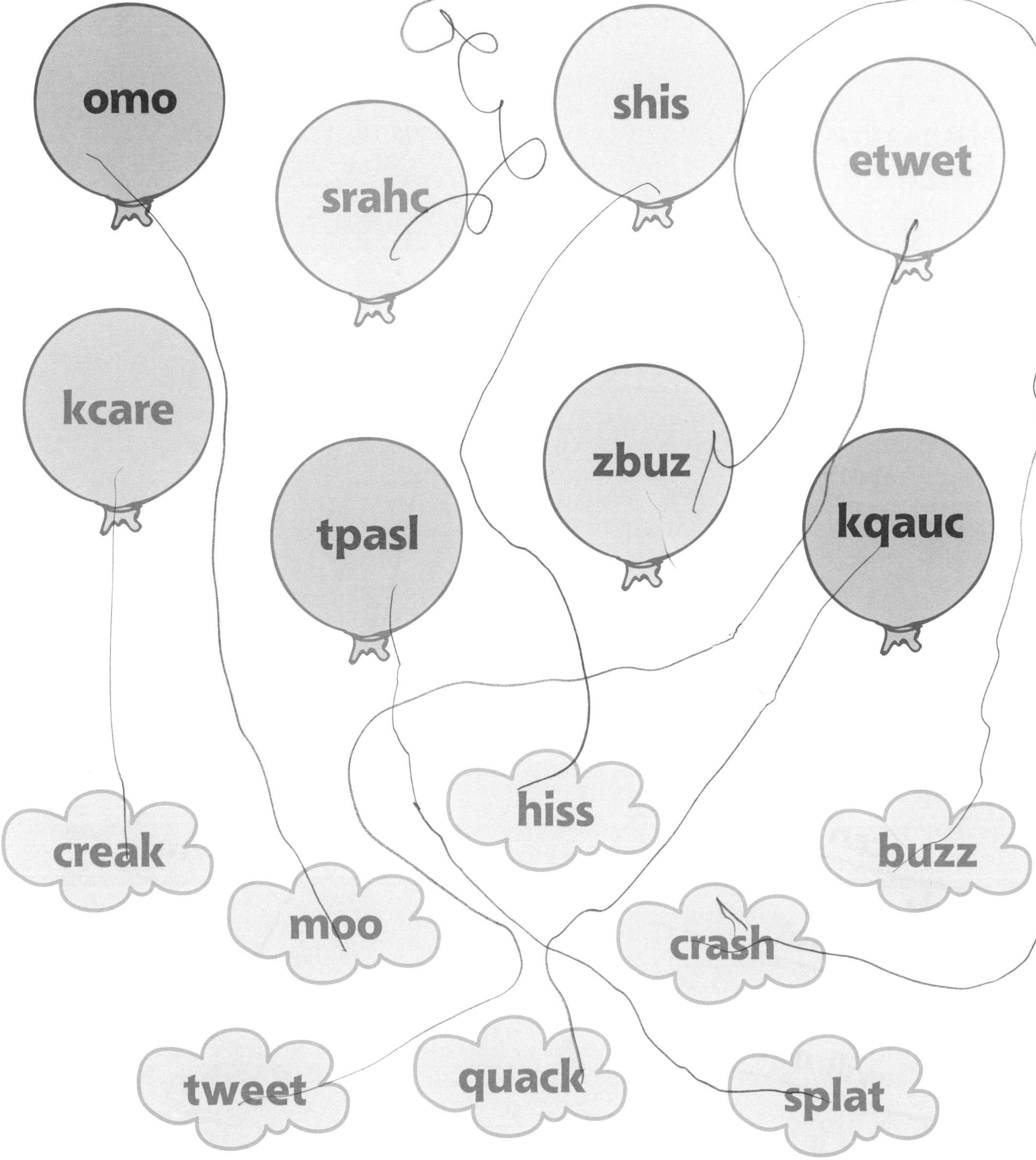

omo

srahc

shis

etwet

kcare

zbuz

kqauc

tpasl

creak

hiss

buzz

moo

crash

tweet

quack

splat

We'll Go Fishing

Uncle Roger wants to take you fishing! He has a special pole for each fish.

Match each pole with the contraction it belongs to. The first one has been done for you.

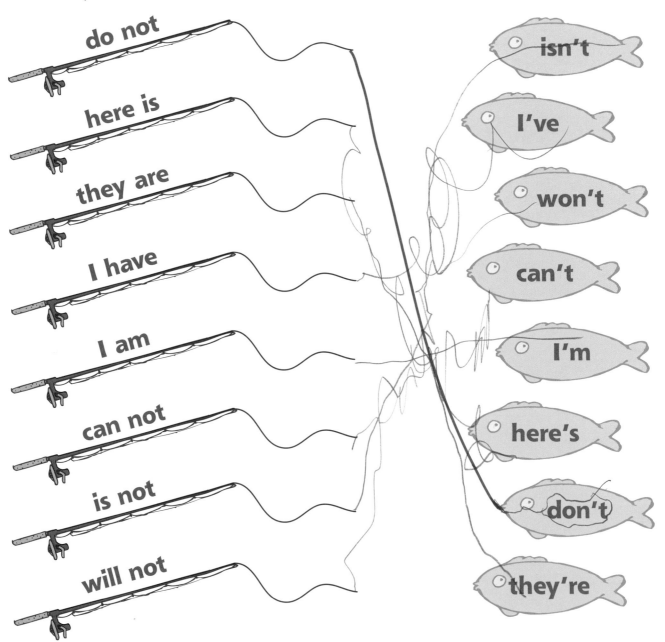

do not

here is

they are

I have

I am

can not

is not

will not

isn't

I've

won't

can't

I'm

here's

don't

they're

32

Dot 2 Dot

Counting by 2s

Follow the dots, counting by 2, until the picture below is through!

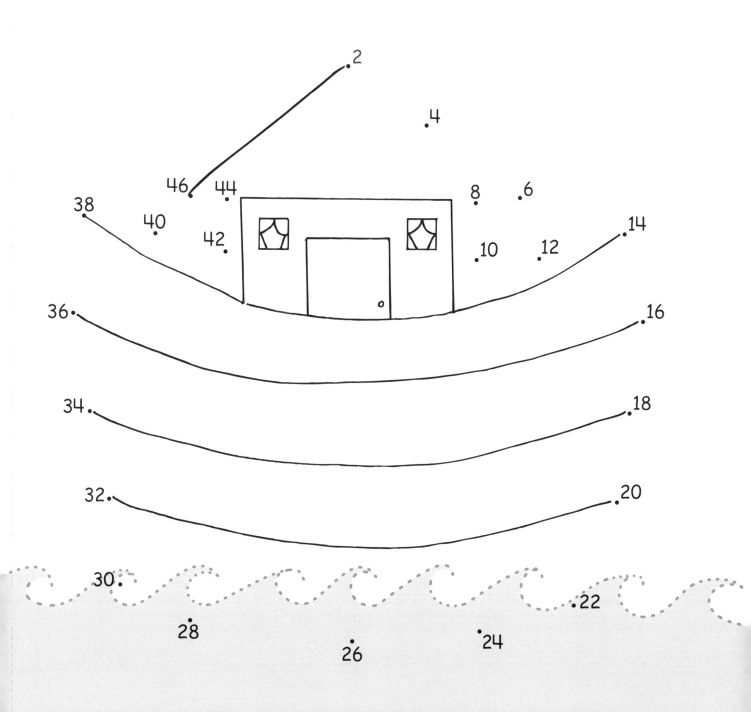

What Animal Are You Like?

Compare yourself with an animal.
Tell how you are like that animal
and in what ways you are different.

34

Nine Fine Fill-ins

Fill in the crossword puzzle using the -in and -ine words in the Word Box.

Across
2. skinny
4. thin rope
5. backbone
7. bottom of a face
9. glow

Down
1. 4 + 5 =
3. a look alike
6. Christmas trees
8. not to lose

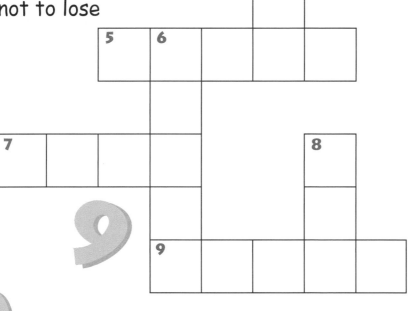
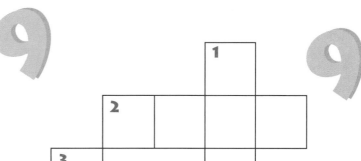

WORD BOX

pines   chin   nine   twin   thin

shine   spine   win   twine

A Penny Saved

Kevin, Ahmed, and Melissa are all saving pennies. They have stacked them in sets of 10.

How many pennies does each person have?

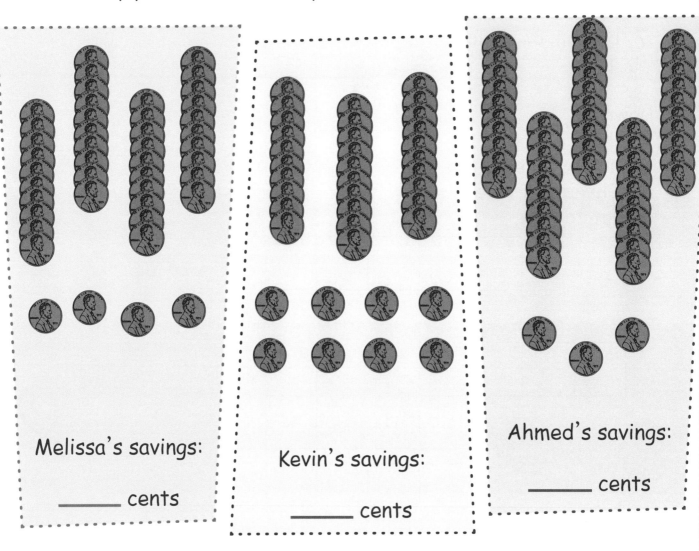

Melissa's savings:

_____ cents

Kevin's savings:

_____ cents

Ahmed's savings:

_____ cents

How much do Ahmed and Kevin have together? _____

How much do Melissa and Ahmed have together? _____

How much do Kevin and Melissa have together? _____

The Spelling Well

Jack and Jill have made a spill.

Their pail of words from the
spelling well have all poured out.

Circle the words that are spelled correctly.
Make an X through the misspelled words.
Then write them correctly on the lines.

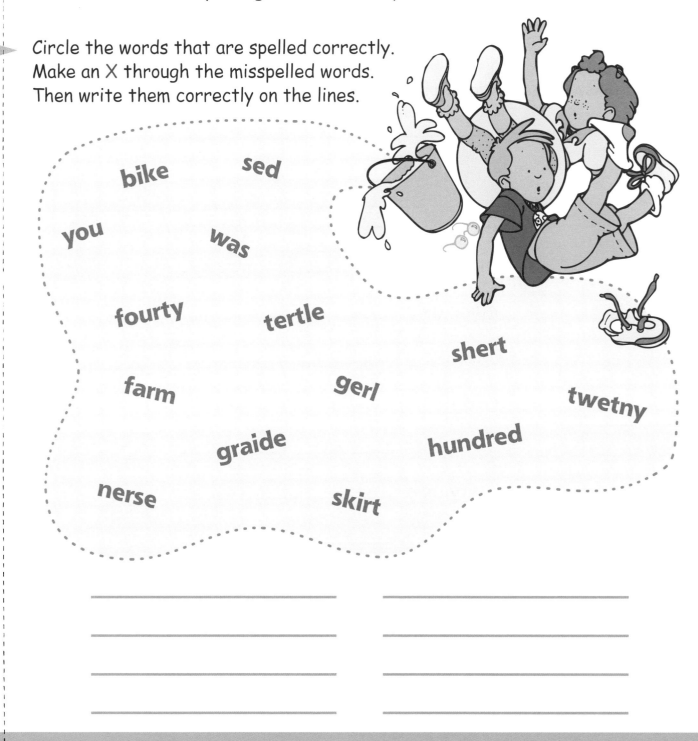

bike

sed

you

was

fourty

tertle

shert

farm

gerl

twetny

graide

hundred

nerse

skirt

_____   _____

_____   _____

_____   _____

_____   _____

Simple Similes

A simile is a phrase using the words **like** or **as**.

easy **as** pie
quiet **as** a mouse

sings **like** a bird
runs **like** the wind

Help finish these similes. Some words in the Word Box may help you.

slippery **as** an _____

fluffy **like** a _____

hungry **as** a _____

quick **as** a _____

swims **like** a _____

cries **like** a _____

loud **as** _____

pretty **as** a _____

smelly **as** a _____

big **as** a _____

WORD BOX

thunder	picture	baby	cloud	skunk
house	fish	bunny	bear	eel

In the Clock Shop

It's 4:35 and almost time to close. Mr. Bell just discovered that his clocks do not have the correct time.

Look at each clock and write the time it is showing. Then on the last clock, draw in the hour and minute hands to show 4:35.

You Say Good-bye; I Say Hello

Big Bob and Little Lee are opposites. If Bob says hello, Lee says good-bye. When Lee says it's cold, Bob says it's hot.

Draw a line from Bob's words on the left to Lee's words on the right.

hello

good-bye

stop	end
right	thin
light	go
loud	bald
fat	wrong
hairy	dark
soft	winter
beginning	quiet
yes	hard
summer	no

Short and Sweet

Some words can be written in a shorter way. These are called **abbreviations**.

Fill in the crossword puzzle below using the complete word for each abbreviation.

Across
2. Dec.
5. qt.
6. in.
7. St.

Down
1. Mr.
2. Dr.
3. cm
4. Rd.

WORD BOX

centimeter	Street	inch	Mister
quart	Doctor	Road	December

Ziggy's Zoo!

Zookeeper Ziggy drew a graph to show how
many of each animal the zoo has.

Read the graph and answer the questions below.

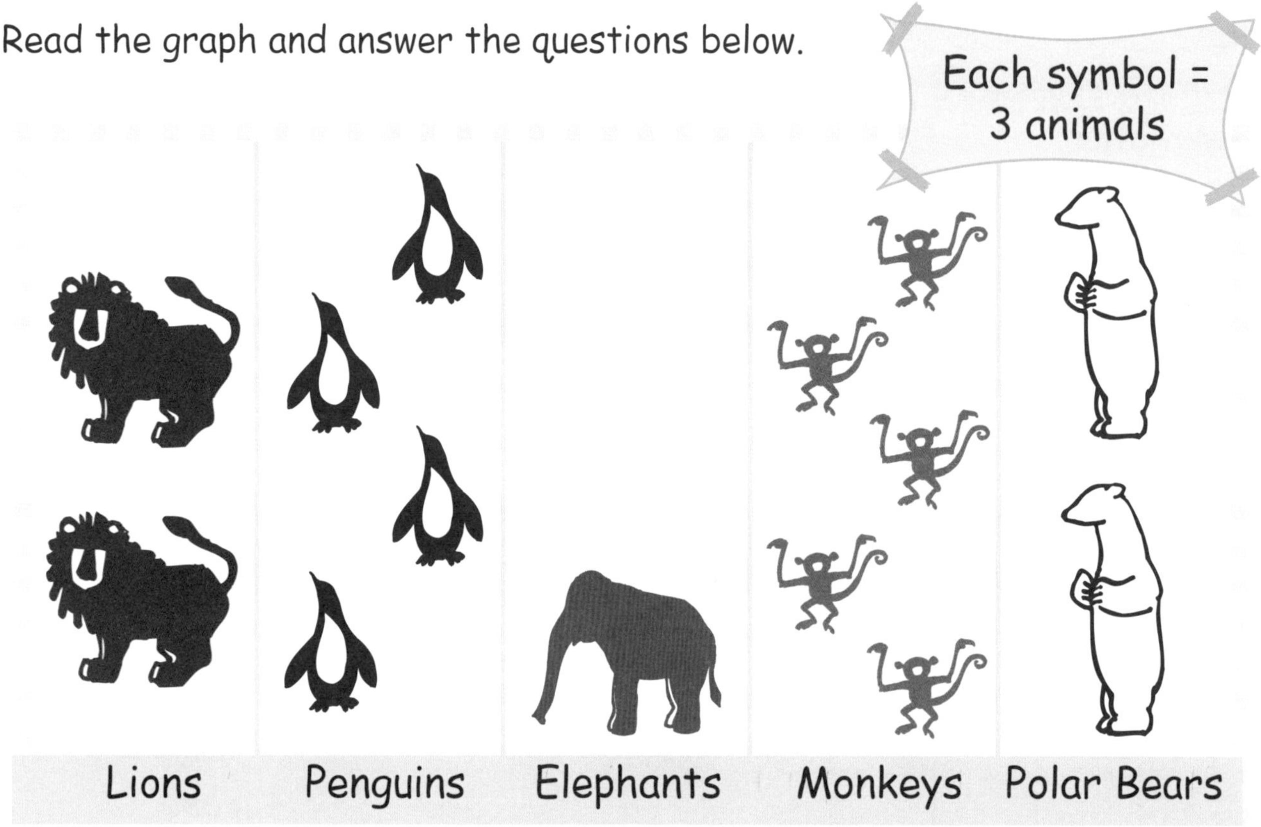

Each symbol =
3 animals

| Lions | Penguins | Elephants | Monkeys | Polar Bears |

1. Which two animals have the same number? _____

   _____

2. How many monkeys are in the zoo? _____

3. How many more penguins are there
   than elephants? _____

4. Are there more penguins or more bears? _____

   How many more? _____

Seasons and Senses

Every season you see, hear, smell, taste, and touch different things. Draw a line from each word to the illustration that tells which sense is used. Some may have more than one answer!

lemon drops

loud bells

soft mittens

fireflies

howling wind

salty seawater

cookies baking

bright fireworks

red hearts

Christmas carols

shiny stars

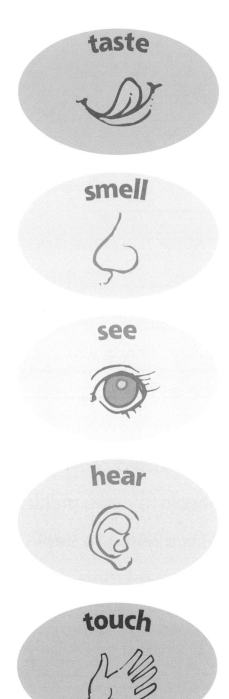

taste

smell

see

hear

touch

43

Drew's Dream

Drew is dreaming of things that begin with the letters dr. Fill in the missing words to tell about Drew's dream.

   Drew dreamed that he sat up in bed. He had heard a noise.

The bottom _____ of his _____ was opening.

Noises were coming from inside it.

   Suddenly the strangest parade you ever saw marched out

of the drawer. Leading the parade was a clown wearing a lacy

_____. As he marched, he waved a _____

to keep the beat. Next to come was a centipede beating a

_____ with his many feet. A funny puppy with short,

little legs and long, _____ ears was third in the parade.

Finally, there was a colorful _____ _____

soda as he _____ a race car.

   The next morning,
Drew vowed to never eat
chocolate and a pickle
before going to bed!

WORD BOX

drill	droopy	drove	dress	dresser
drawer	dragonfly	drum	drinking	

44

Riddle Time

What is big and yellow and has four wheels and flies?

$$\begin{array}{r} 18 \\ -\ 9 \\ \hline 9 \end{array}$$

a

$$\begin{array}{r} 12 \\ -\ 7 \\ \hline \end{array} \quad \begin{array}{r} 14 \\ -\ 5 \\ \hline \end{array} \quad \begin{array}{r} 10 \\ -\ 7 \\ \hline \end{array} \quad \begin{array}{r} 17 \\ -\ 9 \\ \hline \end{array} \quad \begin{array}{r} 12 \\ -\ 3 \\ \hline \end{array} \quad \begin{array}{r} 11 \\ -\ 6 \\ \hline \end{array} \quad \begin{array}{r} 12 \\ -\ 6 \\ \hline \end{array}$$

___ ___ ___ ___ ___ ___

$$\begin{array}{r} 11 \\ -\ 9 \\ \hline \end{array} \quad \begin{array}{r} 12 \\ -\ 9 \\ \hline \end{array} \quad \begin{array}{r} 8 \\ -\ 7 \\ \hline \end{array} \quad \begin{array}{r} 15 \\ -\ 8 \\ \hline \end{array} \quad \begin{array}{r} 12 \\ -\ 8 \\ \hline \end{array}$$

9 – a   6 – e   3 – r
8 – b   5 – g   2 – t
7 – c   4 – k   1 – u

___ ___ ___ ___ ___

Draw the answer here.

Cat-Sitter's Questionnaire

Your new neighbor, Mrs. Whitaker, has a great big cat named Muffy. She may ask you to "cat-sit" sometime if she thinks you would do a good job.

Here are some questions Mrs. Whitaker would like you to answer.

1. What do you like about cats?

2. What don't you like about cats?

3. What would you do if you couldn't find Muffy when you came into the house?

4. What would you do if you ran out of cat food?

Tongue Twisters

When lots of the words in a sentence start with the same sounds, the sentence is hard to say. We call it a tongue twister.

Big bugs bumped Brad badly before breakfast.

Unscramble these words to make some totally terrific tongue twisters!

1. twenty twirled twigs twice

_____

2. grapes Granny grinned gray at

_____

3. played a planet on Paul purple

_____

Now make up your own tongue twisters.

_____

_____

_____

_____

Strike Out the Numbers!

Make an X through the number that does **not** belong in each set below. Then write the correct number. The first one has been done for you.

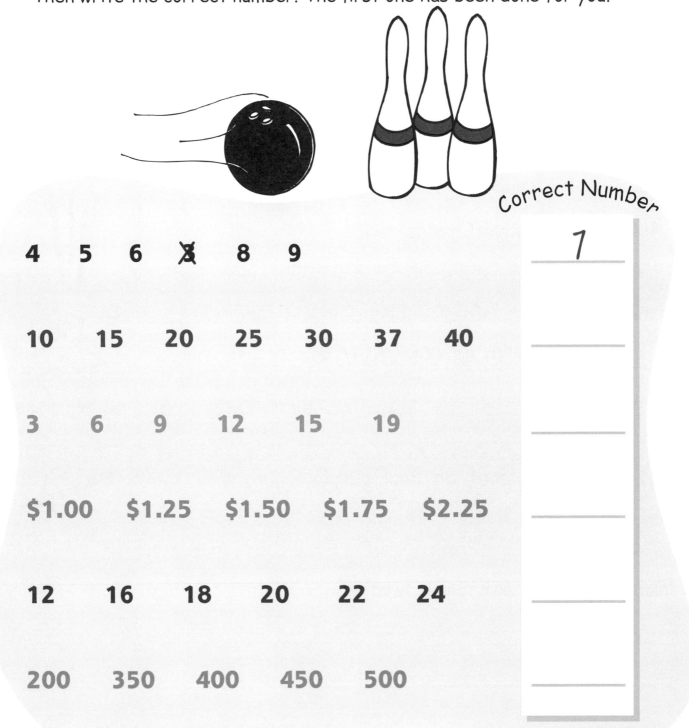

Correct Number

4	5	6	X̶	8	9	7
10	15	20	25	30	37	40
3	6	9	12	15	19	
$1.00	$1.25	$1.50	$1.75	$2.25		
12	16	18	20	22	24	
200	350	400	450	500		

48

Race for the Cheese

Trace the letters to the end of the maze—and the cheese! Trace these words in order:

boy   dog   cat   mouse   cheese

b	o	l	o	g
z	y	d	o	c
e	s	k	t	a
c	u	o	m	y
h	e	w	q	s
b	e	s	e	

Farmer Sam's BIG Trouble

Word Families

What can Farmer Sam do? Something is eating his turnips!

Solve the puzzle and you will find the answer.

fire   __ __ __ __ __
                             3

lives in a shell   __ __ __ __
         5

not wild   __ __ __ __

eggs and _____   __ __ __

what you call yourself   __ __ __ __

sweet potato   __ __ __
               2

like jelly   __ __ __

closing a door hard   __ __ __ __
     4

something to play   __ __ __ __

picture_____   __ __ __ __ __
         1

WORD BOX

slam	game	ham	tame	name
jam	flame	frame	yam	clam

Now write each of the letters with a number on the matching lines below. Then you will have an answer for Farmer Sam.

Tell the __ __ __ to __ __ __ __ __ !
        1   2   3   4   5   1   2   3

I Love Cookies!

Circle how much money I need to buy these cookies.

10¢   5¢

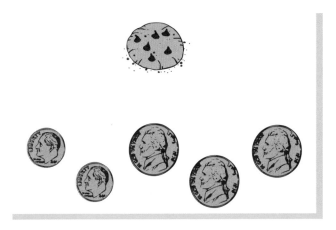

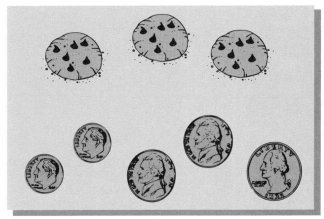

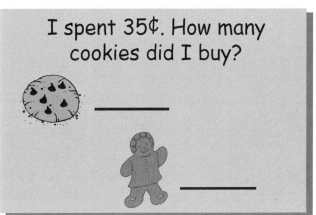

I spent 35¢. How many cookies did I buy?

_____

_____

Terrific Twos

Put two pictures together to make one word. Draw a line from a picture on the left to its second half on the right. Write the new word on the line.

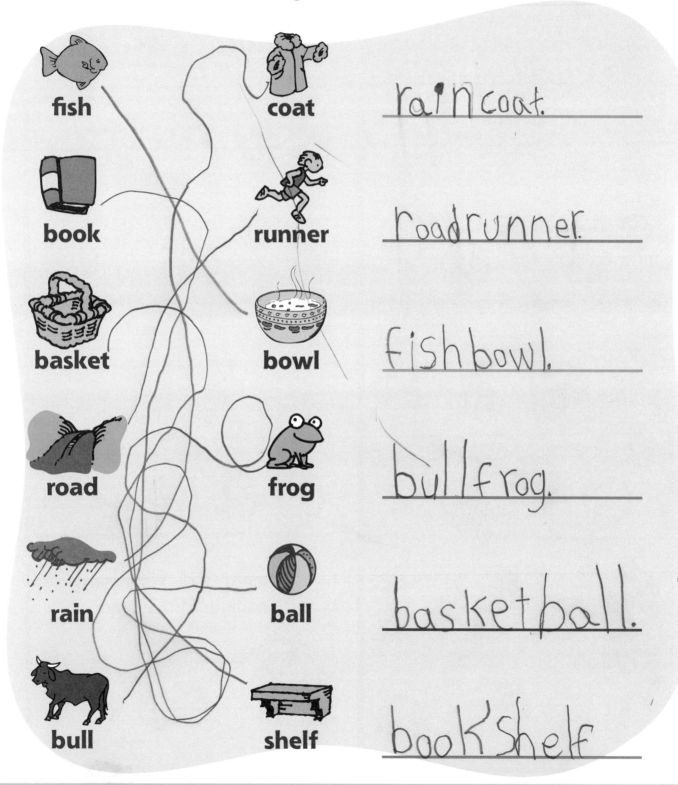

raincoat.

roadrunner.

fishbowl.

bullfrog.

basketball.

bookshelf

Can a Fly Fly in a Can?

Some words are **nouns** (person, place, or thing). Some words are **verbs** (action words). And some words can be **both!**

Color to find the hidden picture.
Color the nouns orange.
Color the verbs green.
Color the words that can be both a noun **and** a verb yellow.

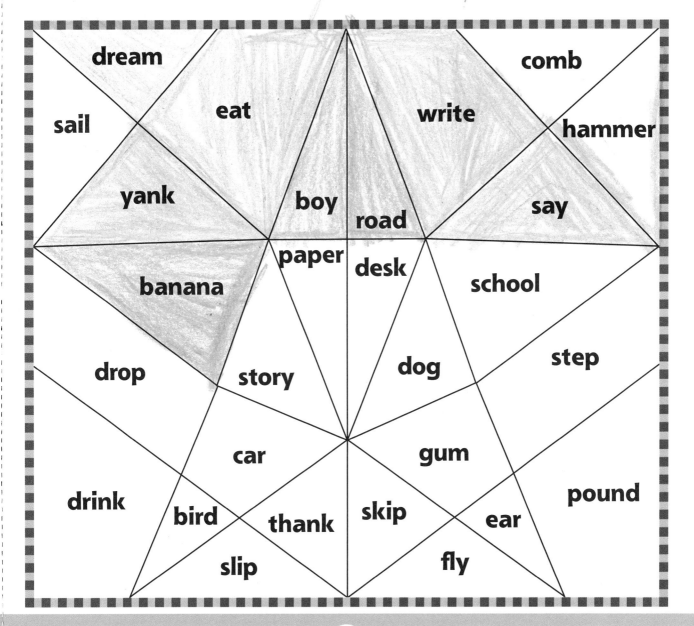

dream

comb

sail

eat

write

hammer

yank

boy

road

say

paper

desk

banana

school

drop

story

dog

step

car

gum

drink

bird

thank

skip

ear

pound

slip

fly

Secret Message

Solve the problems to answer this riddle.

What do you call a cat that loves lemons?

s	r	u	a	u
11		9	8	14
10	10	8	9	16
8	12	8	5	3
+ 6	+ 9	+ 12	+ 7	+ 4

p	s	o	s
11	7	12	10
9	8	10	7
10	15	9	5
+ 9	+ 5	+ 2	+ 13

29	35	33	37	31	39	37	35	35

Shhhhhh! She's Sleeping!

/sh/, /sk/, and /sl/ Blends

Sheri is dreaming about many things.

Fill in the puzzle with the sh, sk, and sl words from her dream.

55

Use Your Senses!

Think about a feeling. Write it in the box below. Then describe that feeling using each of your senses. Here is an example to help you.

Kindness is pale yellow.   (color/see)

It tastes like sweet, cool lemonade.   (taste)

It smells like a spring lilac.   (smell)

It's soft as a baby kitten.   (touch)

It sounds like a lullaby.   (hear)

Kindness is a blue-sky day.   (see)

feeling:

_____ (color/see)

_____ (taste)

_____ (smell)

_____ (touch)

_____ (hear)

_____ (see)

Round and Round We Go

Count by 5s

This toy goes around so fast that it's a blur. Count by 5s and connect the dots to see what it is.

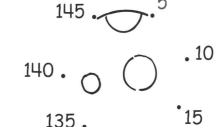

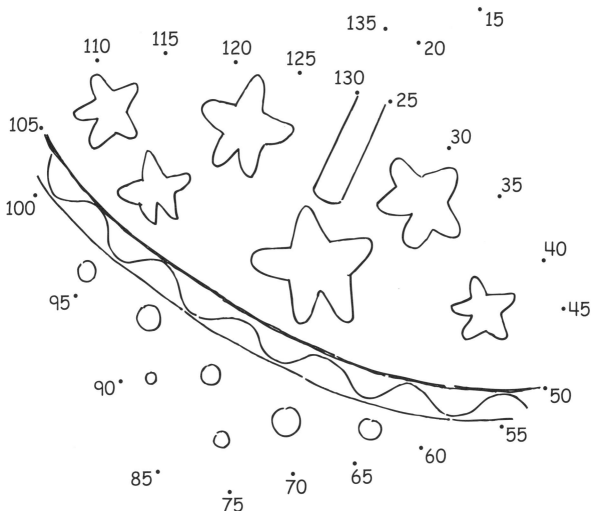

145 ·   · 5
140 ·   · 10
135 ·   · 15
  · 20
110 ·   115 ·   120 ·   125 ·   130 ·   · 25
105 ·   · 30
100 ·   · 35
95 ·   · 40
90 ·   · 45
85 ·   · 50
80 ·   · 55
75 · 70 · 65 · 60

I'm a _____.

Fun in the Sun

Fill in the crossword puzzle below using words from the Word Box.

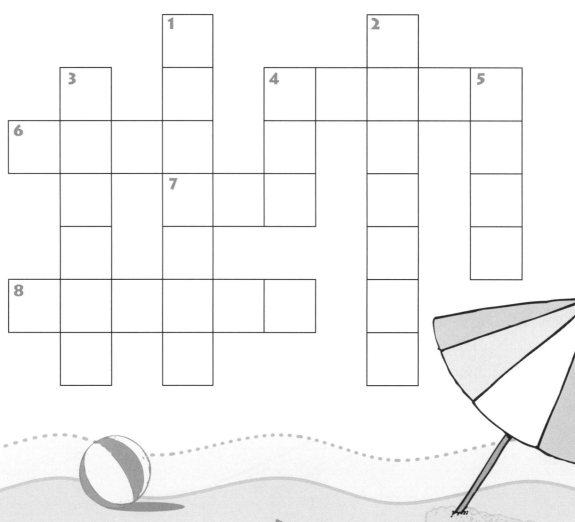

Across

4. walks in the woods
6. lots of these flying around
7. high temperature
8. game with a racquet

Down

1. use a pole and bait to go _____
2. in-line or roller _____
3. the season of the sun
4. wearing one gives you shade
5. fun to do in a pool

WORD BOX

hat	tennis	bugs	skating	summer
hot	fishing	hikes	swim	

My Best Friends

Label the hearts with some of your friends' names. Then fill the hearts with words that tell what makes each friend special.

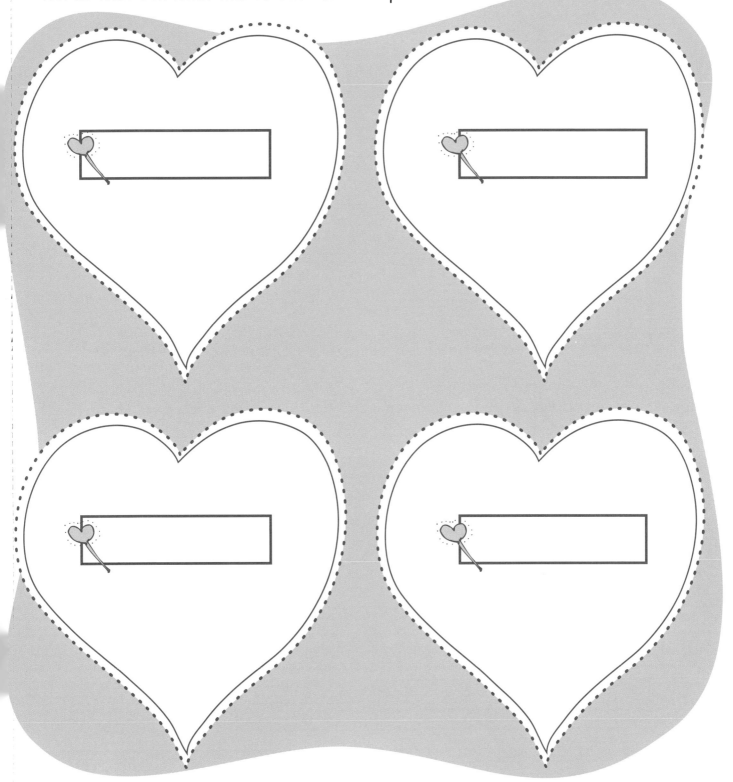

59

What Time Is It?

All of Wayne's watches have stopped. Use the digital clocks to help him set the hands in the correct places.

Which time is Wayne's lunchtime? _____ : _____

Which time is Wayne's bedtime? _____ : _____

It's a Snap!

Put on your thinking cap and help the ape get this crossword puzzle in shape. All the answers will have a short a or a long a.

Across
1. Superman wears a _____
3. _____ are a fruit
5. a circle is a _____
7. an afternoon rest

Down
1. a baseball hat
2. used to catch something
4. to hit
6. a big monkey

Every Body

Look at the pictures below. Each of them is also a body part. Write the word and then draw a line to where it belongs on the body.

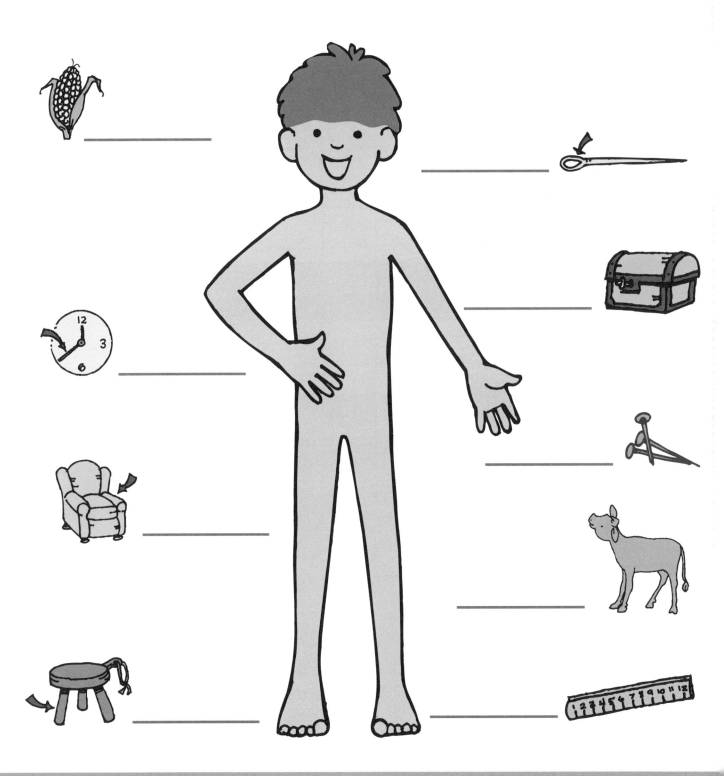

62

Marble Madness

Problem Solving

Four boys are starting a marble collection. Use the clues to tell how many marbles each boy has.

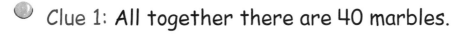

Clue 1: All together there are 40 marbles.

Clue 2: Devon has half of the marbles.

Clue 3: Joe has half of what Devon has.

Clue 4: Mike and Randy each have the same number.

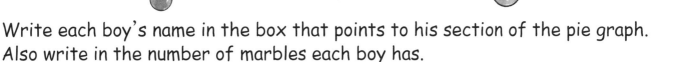

Write each boy's name in the box that points to his section of the pie graph. Also write in the number of marbles each boy has.

Name _____

Number of
Marbles _____

Name _____

Number of
Marbles _____

Name _____

Number of
Marbles _____

Name _____

Number of
Marbles _____

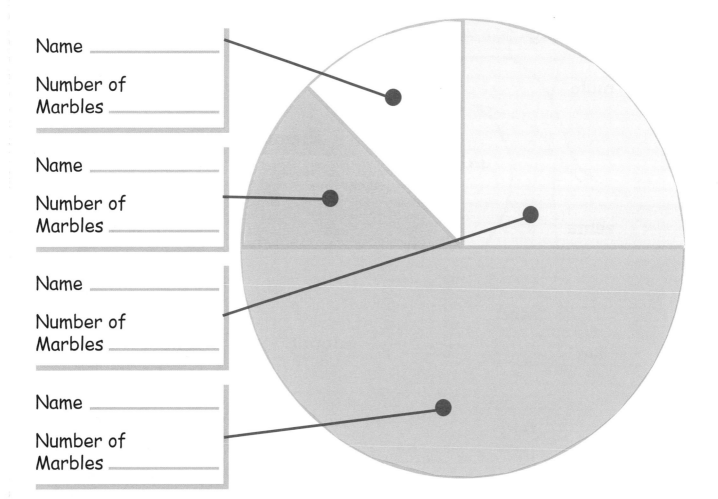

"A" or "An" Tells What I Am

Do you know when to use a and an?
If you can, then you can tell what I am!

If a word begins with a consonant sound, use a.
a tree   a house   a boy

If a word begins with a vowel sound, use an.
an egg   an apple   an igloo

Color words that use a green. Color words that use an gray.

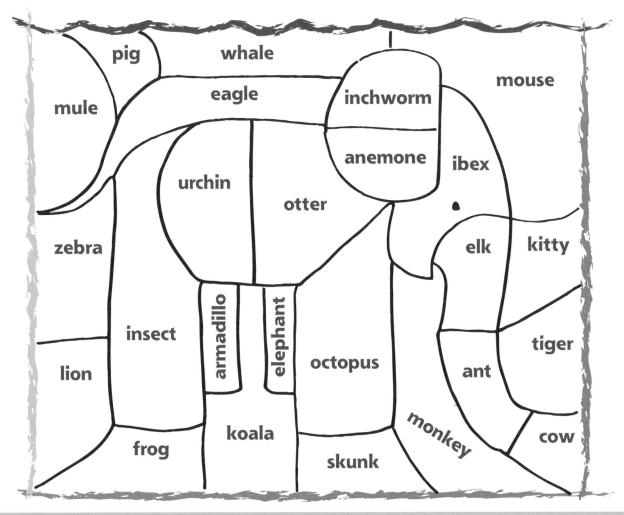

Pick a Pair

Homophones are two words that sound alike but are spelled differently.

Draw lines to make homophone pairs. Then write the pairs of words on the lines below.

1. _____   4. _____

2. _____   5. _____

3. _____   6. _____

At the Pet Store

Use the pictures to answer the questions below about the pets.

1. How many pets does Polly have for sale? _____ pets

2. How many pets are in a container? _____ pets

3. How many four-legged pets are there? _____ pets

4. How many more mammals are there than fish? _____ more

5. Which pet would you want? Why?

_____

_____

Here Kitty, Kitty, Kitty!

Cats love to hide—under the couch, up in a tree, or in a closet. Can you find all of the cat words hiding in the puzzle below? Use the Word Box to help you find all 12 words.

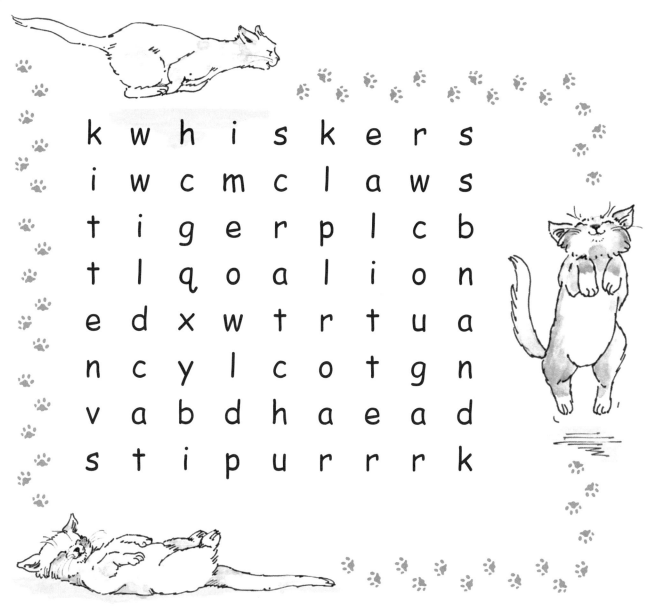

k w h i s k e r s
i w c m c l a w s
t i g e r p l c b
t l q o a l i o n
e d x w t r t u a
n c y l c o t g n
v a b d h a e a d
s t i p u r r r k

WORD BOX

kitten	claws	meow	whiskers	tiger	lion
cougar	roar	purr	wildcat	scratch	litter

Aunt Abby's Attic Alphabet

Aunt Abby has some unusual things in her attic. What do you think she found?

Write at least one thing for each letter of the alphabet.

a _____   n _____

b _____   o _____

c _____   p _____

d _____   q _____

e _____   r _____

f _____   s _____

g _____   t _____

h _____   u _____

i _____   v _____

j _____   w _____

k _____   x _____

l _____   y _____

m _____   z _____

Pick a Lunch!

Ms. Matthews is taking a lunch count.

Complete the bar graph to show how many of each item she counted.

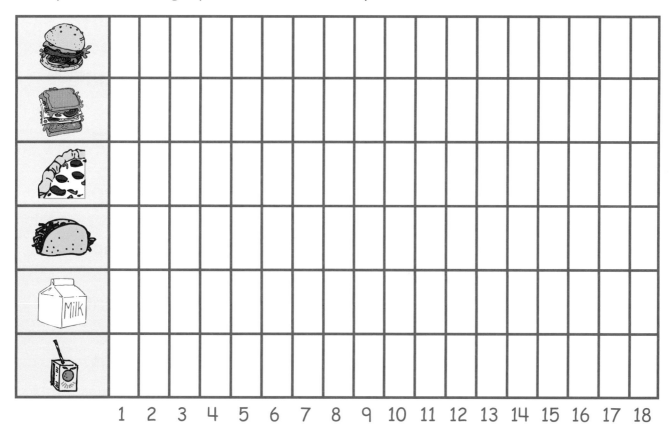

If every student is eating lunch, how many students are in Ms. Matthews' class? _____

Tame Game

Here are some rhyming riddles for you to solve. The correct answer will have two words that rhyme with each other, like this:

unhappy father ⟶ **sad dad**

Draw a line to match the clue on the left with the pair of rhyming words on the right.

violin puzzle	**kitten mitten**
a monkey's superhero cloak	**sandy candy**
not fast frozen drops	**dirt shirt**
beach sweets	**fiddle riddle**
cat's glove	**bug rug**
clothing made of soil	**ape cape**
place to put your toes	**slow snow**
a night animal's cap	**feet seat**
an insect floor covering	**bat hat**

Make up your own rhyming riddle and then answer it.

_____   _____

My Very Own Kingdom

What if you had your own kingdom?
What would you do? How would you feel?

Complete the sentences below to tell how you would rule your very own kingdom.

The name of my kingdom is _____ .

The people would call me _____ .

My castle would be _____ .

My first feast would include _____ .

My royal pet would be _____ .

The kingdom's official colors would be _____ .

I would tell my people _____

_____ .

Here's what my crown would look like:

Button, Button, Who Has a Button?

Betty Jo has lots of buttons. She is using them to learn her fractions. Can you help her out?

Complete the fractions below. The first one has been done for you.

$\dfrac{1}{10}$ of the buttons are round

$\dfrac{}{10}$ of the buttons are square

$\dfrac{}{10}$ of the buttons are blue

$\dfrac{}{10}$ of the buttons are red

$\dfrac{}{10}$ of the buttons are yellow

$\dfrac{}{10}$ of the buttons have 4 holes

$\dfrac{}{10}$ of the buttons have 2 holes

72

Puzzling Palindromes

A palindrome is a word that is spelled the same backward as it is forward.

Find and circle 26 palindromes in the story below. Some are used more than once. The first one has been done for you.

peep!   peep!

One day (Bob) and Anna went to the mountains. Their dad drove until noon. He got tired, so they stopped to buy some pop to drink. Mom waited and waited for Dad to come back to the car. "Toot the horn," said Bob. So she did.

"I'm coming!" called Dad. He gave the pop to Mom.

"I think we're lost," said Anna. She was just playing a gag on Dad.

"Just keep your eye on the map," said Mom. "We'll be fine. Anna sees where we're going."

Soon they were at the river. They rode in a kayak. "Let's have some fun!" said Dad.

And Bob, Anna, Mom, and Dad did!

Do You Want a Bat or a Bat?

Some words look alike but mean different things.

bat   bat

Look at the definitions on each side. Then write the word that is the same in the middle. The first one has been done for you.

group of musicians ___band___ thin rubber strip

beak of a bird _____ paper that tells what is owed

did see _____ cutting tool

finger jewelry _____ bell sound

three feet _____ area around a building

go together _____ stick that makes fire

inside of hand _____ kind of a tree

enclosed area _____ a writing object

WORD BOX
yard   bill   palm   pen   saw   ring   match

Count the Shapes

Match.

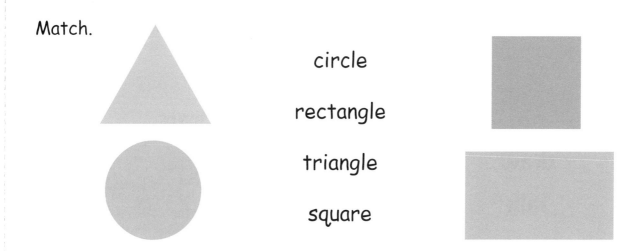

circle

rectangle

triangle

square

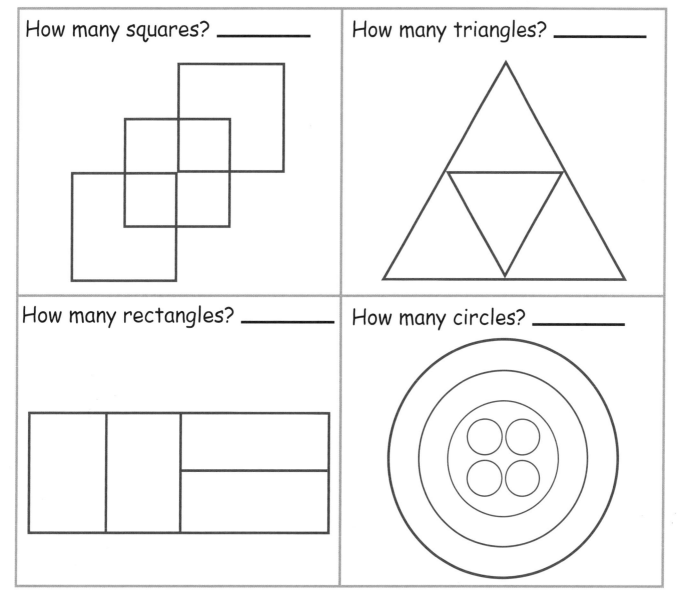

How many squares? _____

How many triangles? _____

How many rectangles? _____

How many circles? _____

75

Match the Action

Draw a line to match the action words (verbs) with their synonyms (words that mean the same).

run	drag
draw	giggle
talk	purchase
laugh	leap
yell	tremble
jump	chat
pull	sob
eat	shout
cry	capture
catch	sketch
buy	gallop
shake	nibble

Can you run as fast as a horse can gallop?

_____

I Won't Do It!

Change the underlined words in the story to contractions. Use the contractions in the Word Box. The first one has been done for you.

Lisa <u>is not</u> happy. Today is her dance

recital. <u>She is</u> upset! Maybe Lisa is just

nervous. She told her mom that she <u>will not</u>

dance. "<u>I am</u> not going to do it!" said Lisa.

"And you <u>cannot</u> make me."

"<u>We will</u> see," said her mom. Soon they

drove off. "<u>Let us</u> just think about all the

fun <u>you have</u> had," she told Lisa.

"<u>That is</u> the thing to do."

Soon Lisa was at the recital. "<u>I have</u>

had fun dancing," Lisa thought. "Maybe <u>I will</u>

give it a try." And she did.

"<u>You are</u> a good dancer," everyone told

Lisa. "<u>What is</u> your secret?"

"I <u>cannot</u> tell you," she answered. Then

she smiled.

isn't

_____

_____

_____

_____

_____

_____

_____

_____

_____

_____

_____

_____

WORD BOX

| I'll | you're | won't | let's | you've | that's | isn't |
| can't | she's | I've | what's | I'm | we'll | |

Yard Sale Today!

Lena, Bill, Mark, and Sally are going to the Big City Summer Yard Sale.

Look at all of the items for sale. Tell how much each person spent.

Receipt

Lena bought the kangaroo toy and candle.

She spent _____ ¢.

Bill bought the baseball and pencil.

He spent _____ ¢.

Mark bought the hat and comic book.

He spent _____ ¢.

Sally bought the bank and mitten.

She spent _____ ¢.

Who spent the most money? _____

Which two people spent the same amount? _____

Recipe for a Sandwich

Create a new, yummy sandwich. Draw a diagram to show its layers. Then write a recipe for all those who would like to try it out.

diagram:

My Sandwich

I named it:

_____

You will need:

_____   _____

_____   _____

_____   _____

Here's how to make it:

_____

_____

_____

_____

_____

Words on the Move

wiggle  flutter strut

wobble twist gallop
wobble

Some verbs aren't for standing still. With your body, show what the words above mean. Then find other verbs for moving. Make a list of them here.

_____	_____
_____	_____
_____	_____
_____	_____

Use some of your moving words to describe an animal.

_____

_____

_____

_____

With a twist of her body, the cat wiggled out of my arms and leaped away.

Riddle Time

Two-Digit Addition and Subtraction

The more we dry, the wetter we get.

(93 t) (56 w) (61 b) (90 s) (77 a)

(80 h) (70 e) (26 o) (38 l)

Add or subtract. Write the letter that goes with each answer.

22 +39 61	86 - 9	37 +56	52 +28

48 +45	93 -67	84 -28	55 +15	70 -32	87 + 3

b _ _ _ _   _ _ _ _ _ _

Rhyme Time

Look at the pictures below. How many words can you think of that rhyme with each one?

rose

_____ _____

_____ _____

_____ _____

_____ _____

☐ words

nail

_____ _____

_____ _____

_____ _____

_____ _____

☐ words

bee

_____ _____

_____ _____

_____ _____

_____ _____

☐ words

dog

_____ _____

_____ _____

_____ _____

_____ _____

☐ words

Rainy Day Riddles

Read the riddle in each puddle. Write the answer on the line.

The things I weave you cannot wear. You could not use my thread to sew on a button.

I am a _____ .

I am like a white sheep grazing in a blue field. When the wind comes, I move away fast.

I am a _____ .

The more you use me the smaller I get. One end rubs off what my other end makes.

I am a _____ .

Put me in and out through round holes. Then tie a bow and away we'll go.

I am a _____ .

Stick the Stamps

Each of the packages below needs stamps. Draw a line from the package to its correct group of stamps. You will need to add to find each answer.

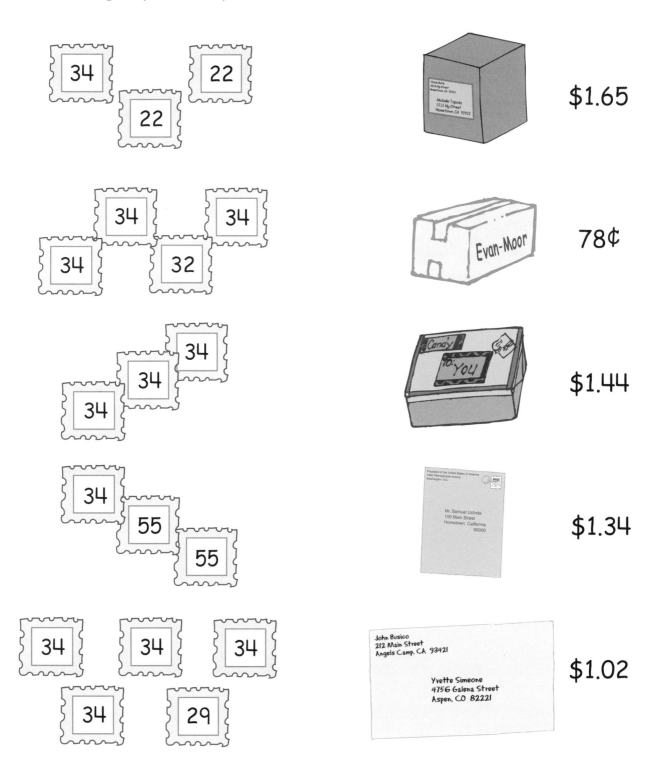

84

Strange Soup

Welcome to the Super Soup Restaurant!
All they serve is soup—and strange soup, too!

Look at the words in each bowl and name the strange soup. The first one has been done for you.

sparrow   robin
crow   blue jay

___bird___
soup

fly   grasshopper
cricket   ant

_____
soup

penny   dime
quarter   nickel

_____
soup

banana   apple
grapes   peach

_____
soup

gumdrop   jelly bean
chocolate   lollipop

_____
soup

rose   daisy
daffodil   tulip

_____
soup

Sally's Spill

Sally Synonym dropped all her words down the stairs. Write the word that means the same as the word on each step. Use the Word Box below.

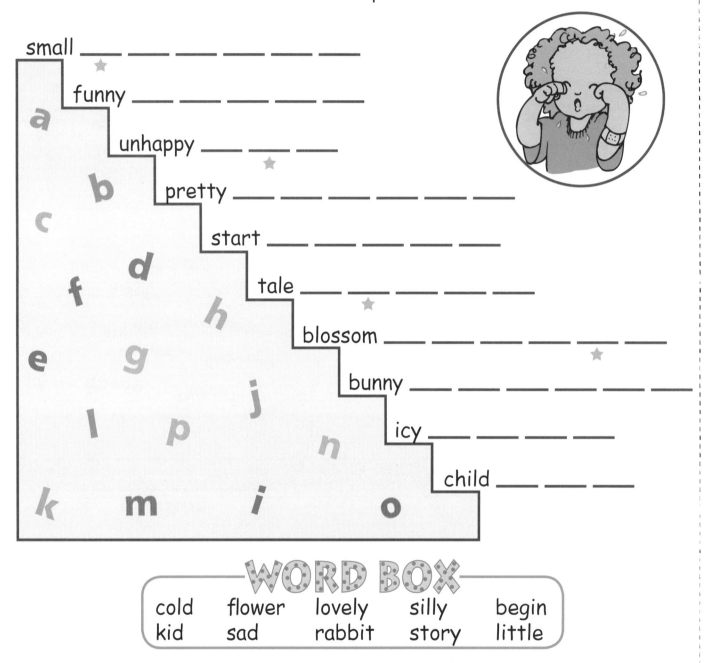

small ___ ___ ___ ___ ___ ___

funny ___ ___ ___ ___ ___

unhappy ___ ___ ___

pretty ___ ___ ___ ___ ___ ___

start ___ ___ ___ ___ ___

tale ___ ___ ___ ___ ___

blossom ___ ___ ___ ___ ___ ___

bunny ___ ___ ___ ___ ___ ___

icy ___ ___ ___ ___

child ___ ___ ___

WORD BOX

cold	flower	lovely	silly	begin
kid	sad	rabbit	story	little

Now write each of the starred (★) letters in order on the lines below to solve this riddle:

What do you call someone whose watch is broken? ___ ___ ___ ___ ___

Busy, Busy Garden

Fill in the blanks. Complete the fraction in each box. There are 8 insects in all.

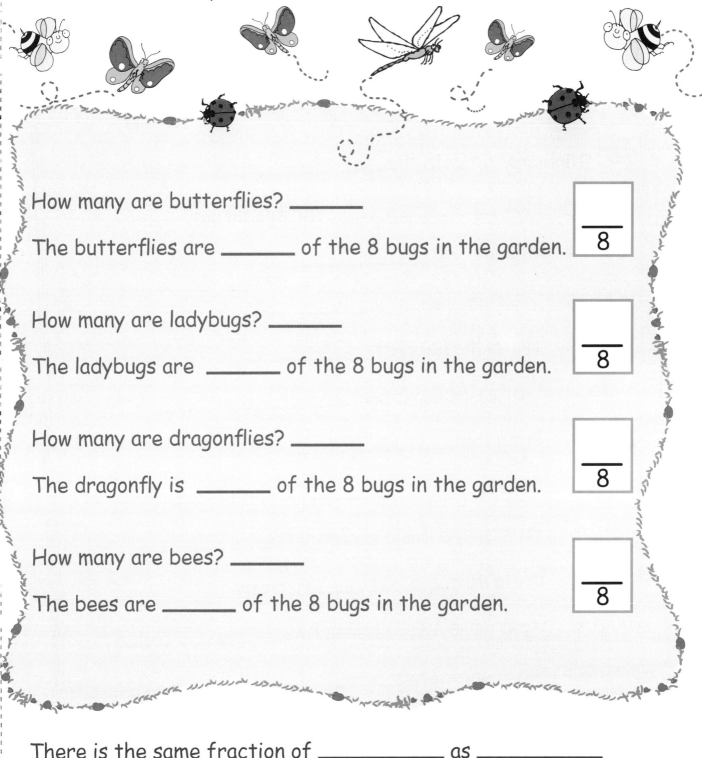

How many are butterflies? _____

The butterflies are _____ of the 8 bugs in the garden. ⬜/8

How many are ladybugs? _____

The ladybugs are _____ of the 8 bugs in the garden. ⬜/8

How many are dragonflies? _____

The dragonfly is _____ of the 8 bugs in the garden. ⬜/8

How many are bees? _____

The bees are _____ of the 8 bugs in the garden. ⬜/8

There is the same fraction of _____ as _____ in the garden.

Betsy Bee's Busy Day

Betsy Bee has so much to do!
She has her whole day planned out.

Fill in the blanks to tell about Betsy's day.

7:00 a.m.   Get up with the _____.

8:00 a.m.   Eat _____ for breakfast.

9:00 a.m.   Sharpen my _____.

10:00 a.m.   Clean my bee _____.

11:00 a.m.   Fly to the nearest _____.

Noon   Gather pollen from the _____.

1:00 p.m.   Bring the _____ her lunch.

2:00 p.m.   Take a _____. Z-Z-Z-Z-Z-Z

3:00 p.m.   Turn on the music and practice my _____.

4:00 p.m.   Invite my _____ over.

5:00 p.m.   Enjoy more sweet honey for _____.

WORD BOX

dance   sun   honey   dinner   flowers   queen
hive   nap   garden   friends   stinger

Silly Salad

Chef Sherman is putting together a very silly salad.
Help him choose what goes into his newest recipe.

Fill in each blank using a word of the same color.

Silly Salad

Recipe ingredients:

3 wiggly [_____]

5 moldy [_____]

4 fuzzy [_____]

1 cup of pretty [_____]

2 exploding [_____]

Mix the first two ingredients in a [_____] bowl.

Stir them until the salad looks [_____]. Then chop

up the last three ingredients until the whole bowl looks like

[_____] [_____]. When you smell the

[_____], it's time to toss the salad.

Do You Have Change for a V?

Jon Jones likes to use Roman numerals when he writes. Can you tell what number each Roman numeral stands for? Write your answer in the box.

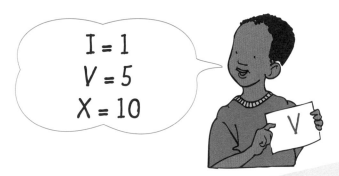

I = 1
V = 5
X = 10

Jon's birthday is October VII.   October ☐

☐ Maple Street

Jon's address is XVI Maple Street.

Jon's favorite number is XI.   number ☐

Jon's older brother is XIII years old.   ☐ years old

Jon has XXVII dollars in his bank.   ☐ dollars

Jon has XXXIII marbles in his collection.   ☐ marbles

Bonus

Jon's phone number is:
III V II – VI V I VIII   ....

String Thing

Follow the kitty's string and fill in all of the str- words from knot to knot.

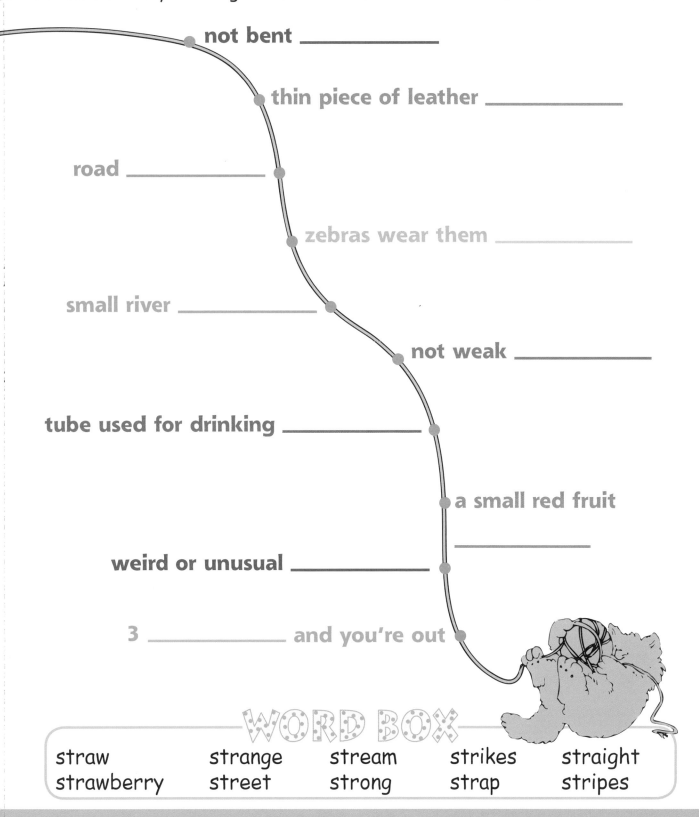

not bent _____

thin piece of leather _____

road _____

zebras wear them _____

small river _____

not weak _____

tube used for drinking _____

a small red fruit

_____

weird or unusual _____

3 _____ **and you're out**

WORD BOX

straw	strange	stream	strikes	straight
strawberry	street	strong	strap	stripes

91

Through the Trees

/tr/, /thr/ Blends

We are going for a walk through the woods. As we walk along, we will see lots of things that begin with tr- and thr-.

Use words from the Word Box to fill in the crossword puzzle.

Across
1. used for sewing
4. farmers use this
6. to take a chance
7. 8 minus 5

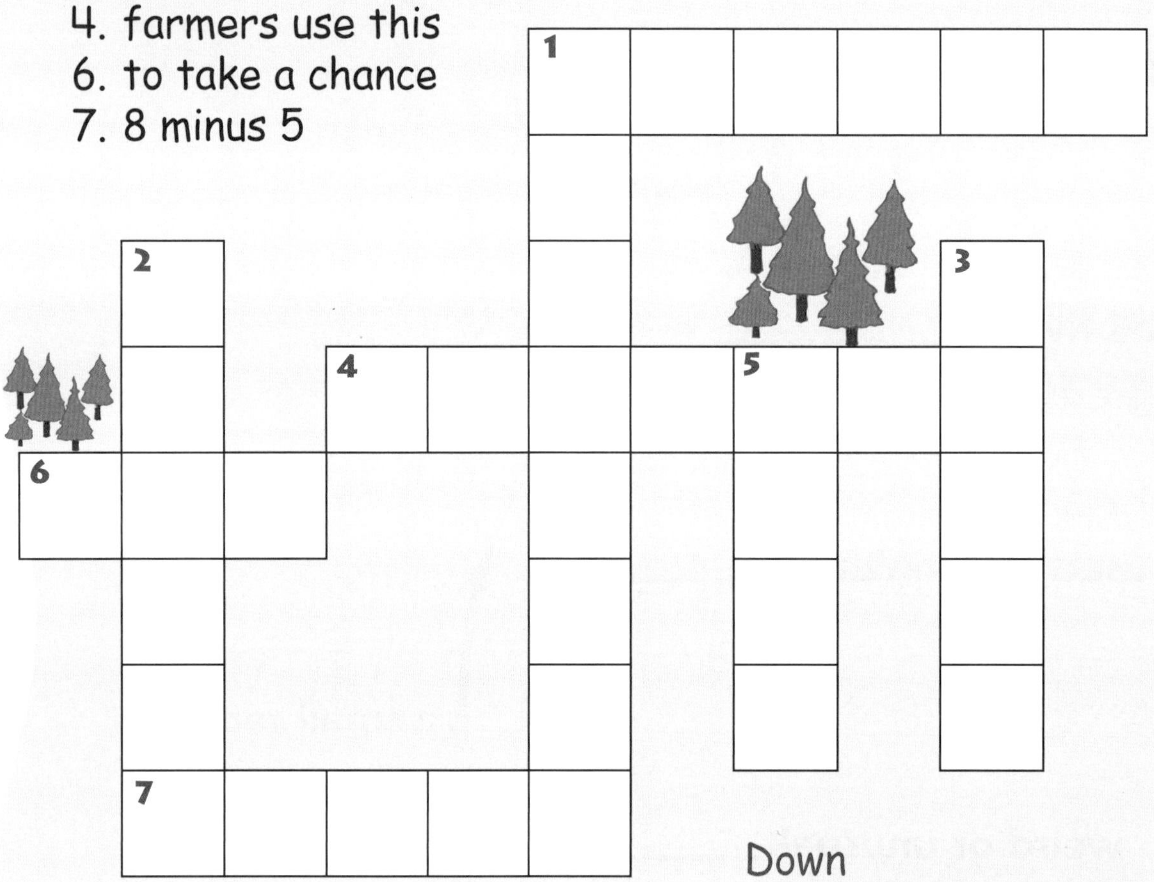

Down
1. it has three sides
2. part of your neck
3. part of a railroad
5. not false

WORD BOX

true	thread	tractor	throat
three	triangle	try	track

Aunt Betsy's Bakery

Subtraction

Aunt Betsy has the best bakery! At the end of the day, she has to count the baked goods below to see what is left. Can you help her?

Aunt Betsy started the day with the amounts below. How many of each did she sell?

16 doughnuts _____ sold   12 sugar cookies _____ sold

5 pies _____ sold   7 gingerbread boys _____ sold

12 cupcakes _____ sold   12 chocolate cookies _____ sold

How many sold?

doughnuts + pies = _____ sold

cupcakes + sugar cookies = _____ sold

gingerbread boys + chocolate cookies = _____ sold

gingerbread boys + pies = _____ sold

doughnuts + cupcakes = _____ sold

Join the Club

The students at Midtown School want to start
some clubs. But they need help naming them.

Match each name choice to the club it would fit. Circle the name you would
choose for each club.

Name		Club

Comets

Decimals

Slam Dunks

Wild Cats

Scissors-n-Thread

Galaxies

Home Runs

Bear Buddies

Fractions

Needles and Pins

Sports Club

Math Club

Animal Lovers' Club

Sewing Club

Space Club

Dear Diary

Pretend this is a page in your diary. Write about a good day you have had.

Dear Diary,

What a day this was!

Your friend,

A Word's Worth

Add to find out what each word is worth. The first one has been done for you.

a = 1¢	e = 5¢	i = 9¢	m = 13¢	q = 17¢	u = 21¢	y = 25¢
b = 2¢	f = 6¢	j = 10¢	n = 14¢	r = 18¢	v = 22¢	z = 26¢
c = 3¢	g = 7¢	k = 11¢	o = 15¢	s = 19¢	w = 23¢	
d = 4¢	h = 8¢	l = 12¢	p = 16¢	t = 20¢	x = 24¢	

fun __6¢__ + __21¢__ + __14¢__ = __41¢__   sat ____ + ____ + ____ = _____

eat ____ + ____ + ____ = _____   mop ____ + ____ + ____ = _____

boy ____ + ____ + ____ = _____   web ____ + ____ + ____ = _____

red ____ + ____ + ____ = _____   lip ____ + ____ + ____ = _____

Draw a picture of the word that is worth the most.

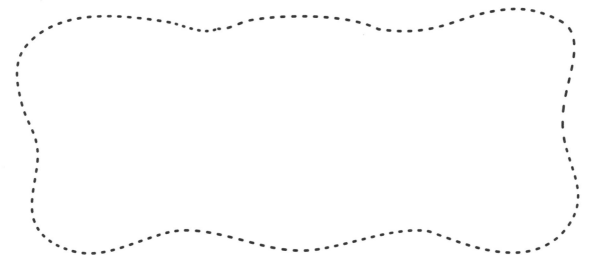

What Was That?

The punctuation marks are missing from this story. Put them back.

. , ? !

Fred Frog lived in a big pond   He liked to croak swim and eat flies all day long   One day a loud sound woke Fred from a nap Splash Fred jumped   Where did that sound come from   Splash Splash   Splash   It was getting closer   Fred looked all around   Then he looked on the shore   There it was   Splash   Splash   Was it something scary   No it was just a small freckle-faced boy skipping rocks in the water   Fred went back to his nap

97

How Do They Compare?

Look at each column of three pictures. One of the pictures has the correct word next to it. Add er or est to the other two words.

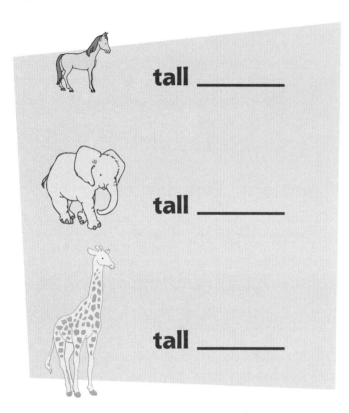

tall _____

tall _____

tall _____

young _____

young _____

young _____

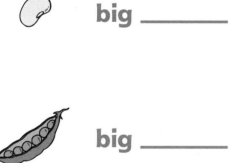

big _____

big _____

big _____

small _____

small _____

small _____

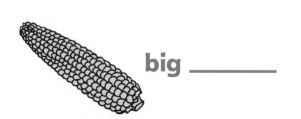

Crazy About Crayons

Greater Than, Less Than, Equal To

Use this graph to compare the number of crayons the children have.
Use one of these symbols in each box below.

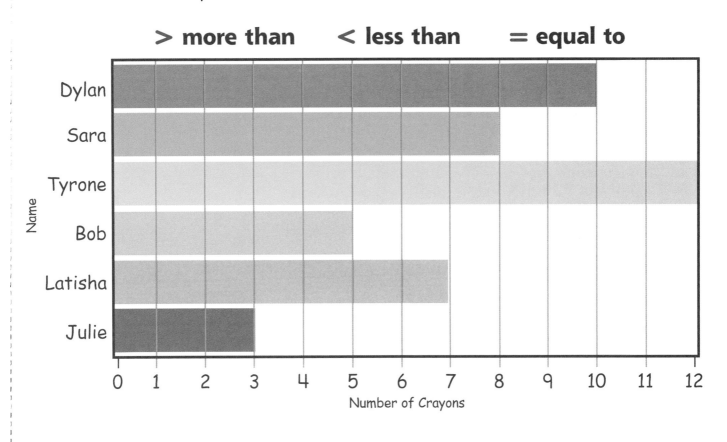

> **more than**   < **less than**   = **equal to**

Dylan		Latisha
Sara		Tyrone
Bob		Julie
Julie + Latisha		Dylan
Bob + Julie		Dylan + Latisha
Sara + Tyrone		Julie + Dylan

First, Next, and Last

Stories happen in order. First . . . next . . . last!

I got money from my bank.

I went to the ice-cream man.

I bought a cherry Popsicle.

First   **Next**   **Last**

Draw your own story in order. Then tell about each part.

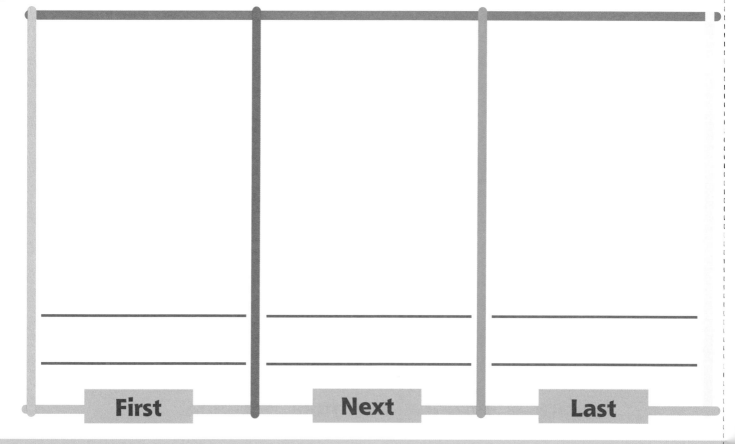

First   **Next**   **Last**

Feeling Tip Top

Connect the dots next to the ow words in alphabetical order. Then fill in the ow words in the poem.

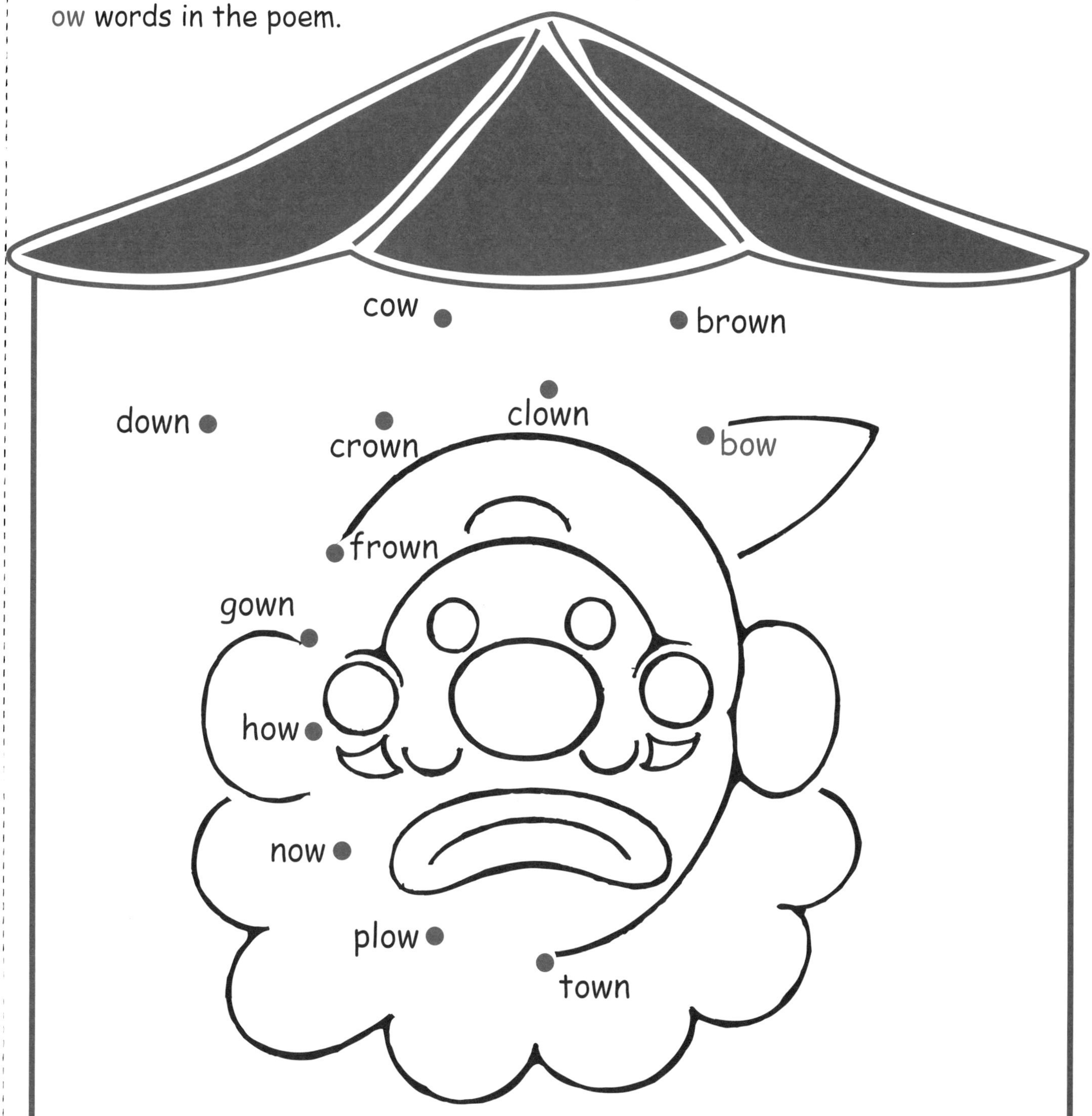

cow •

• brown

down •

• crown

clown

• bow

• frown

gown •

how •

now •

plow •

town

This is Tops, the circus _____.

Turn his _____ upside _____.

Ride the Rainbow

Count by the number at the beginning of each color. Fill in all of the blanks to make it to the gold at the end.

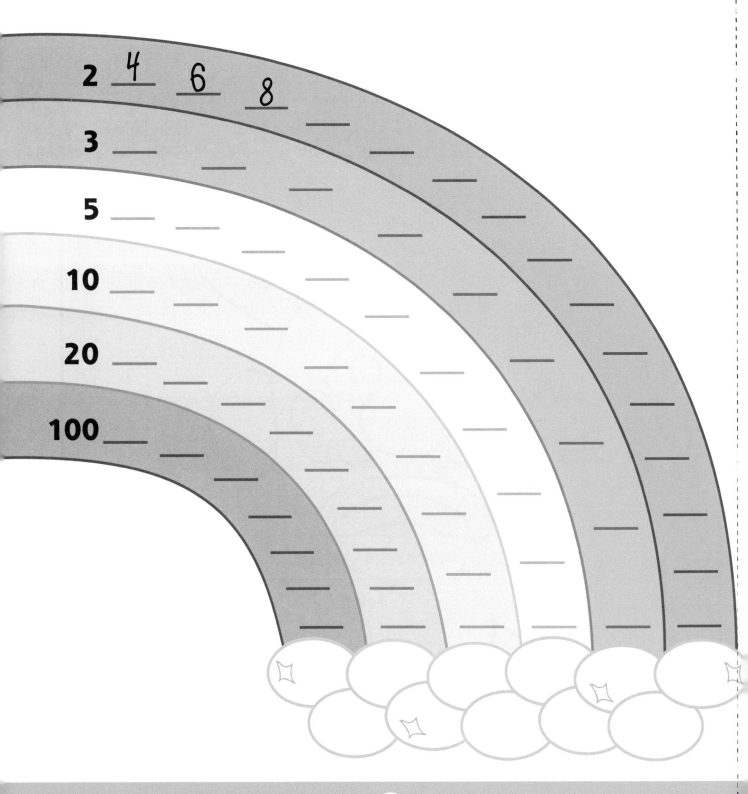

2   _4_   _6_   _8_

3

5

10

20

100

Connect Two!

Write the name of each picture to make a compound word. Then draw a picture of the new word. The first one has been done for you.

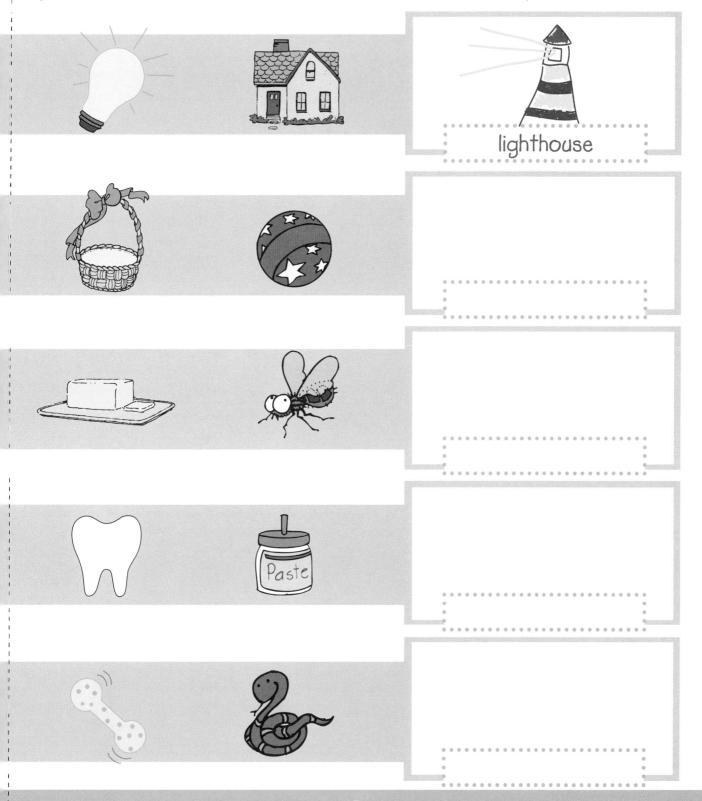

lighthouse

Teeny Tiny Tennis Tournament

Descriptive Writing

Here is a special tennis tournament. Pretend you are a sports reporter and write all about the tournament.

Down by the Sea

Todd and his sister Rachel saw lots of things down by the sea. Add up all the things they saw.

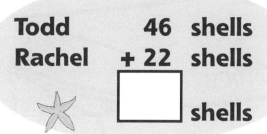

Todd   46   shells
Rachel   + 22   shells

☐ shells

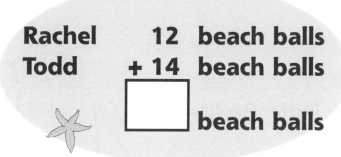

Rachel   12   beach balls
Todd   + 14   beach balls

☐ beach balls

Rachel   23   sea gulls
Todd   + 15   sea gulls

☐ sea gulls

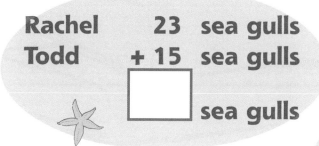

Rachel   13   beach towels
Todd   + 18   beach towels

☐ beach towels

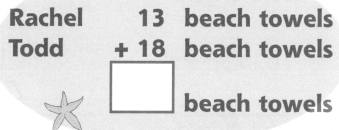

Todd   87   waves
Rachel   + 65   waves

☐ waves

Todd   39   gum wrappers
Rachel   + 18   gum wrappers

☐ gum wrappers

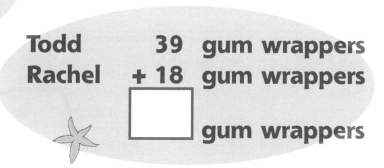

Which items should be put in the nearest trash can? Circle that problem.

A Book Collection

Tyler and his sister Teresa have a big book collection! But they are not in any order. Put the books in alphabetical order from top to bottom. Draw a line to the correct place. Then write the title on the book. The first one has been done for you.

Pink Pandas

Little Bo Peep

Go, Dog, Go

Turtle Soup

Bambi

Real-Life Race Cars

Snow White

Cats Are Curious

Heidi

A Pink Mink?

Here are some rhyming riddles for you to solve. The correct answer will have two words that rhyme with each other, like this:

What do you call a furry animal that gets washed with a red sock?

a pink mink

Match the riddle on the left with the correct answer on the right.

a brightly colored place to sleep	teal seal
sunny, wiggly food	white kite
a flying toy the color of snow	gray day
blue-green sea mammal	brown clown
a dark bag	red bed
grass-colored vegetable	blue shoe
chocolate funny man	yellow Jell-O
gloomy weather	black sack
denim-colored footware	green bean

107

Super Candy Sale!

Wow! The students at Southside School have sold a bunch of candy. Use the clues below to fill in the chart with the correct amounts.

	Amy	Malcolm	Zoe	Hiroshi	Total
bags of jelly beans					
candy bars					
extra-big lollipops					
tins of taffy					

Clues

1. Zoe sold 5 of each: bags of jelly beans, candy bars, lollipops, and taffy.

2. Amy sold 3 more bags of jelly beans and lollipops than Zoe.

3. Malcolm sold 2 fewer of taffy and 1 more of candy bars than Zoe.

4. Hiroshi sold the same number of bags of jelly beans as Amy.

5. Hiroshi and Malcolm sold the same number of lollipops as Zoe.

6. Amy sold no taffy, but she sold 4 more candy bars than Malcolm.

7. Hiroshi sold the amount of taffy that Zoe and Malcolm sold **added together**.

8. Hiroshi sold 8 fewer candy bars than Amy.

9. Malcolm sold the same amount of bags of jelly beans as he did of taffy.

10. The total amount of all the candy sold was 86 items.

Bonus  If the school made $2.00 for each item sold, how much money did it make?

Thanks a Bunch!

Millie wrote a nice thank-you note to her aunt for her birthday present. The words in red print will give you clues about what the birthday present was. Use the Word Box to help you unscramble the words.

Dear Aunt Clara,

[_____]

Thank you so much for the zmaigna present. I was so surprised to

[_____]

see its srkeihsw poking out of the box. Then I opened it. Your present

[_____] [_____] [_____] [_____]

was ruyfr and ivale! It had a long lita and pink yees. I am so glad you

[_____] [_____]   [_____]

also gave me a geac and lehwe for it, too. I like to feed it escehe and

[_____]   [_____]

dsese. At first Mom was afraid of it. But once it lwigdeg its little

[_____]

seon at her, she was fine.

[_____]

Thanks again for my wonderful little umeso.

Your loving niece,

Millie

WORD BOX

cheese	eyes	nose	furry	amazing	alive
whiskers	cage	tail	seeds	wiggled	wheel

Millie's present was a _____ .

109

Fun with Fill-ins!

Choose any word from the same color group to write in each blank. Make a funny or real story. It's up to you!

Nouns
(naming words)

treasure	cookies
snowman	river
cave	doughnuts
garbage	puddle
bunnies	cactus
mountain	skunk

Verbs
(action words)

woke	dig
got	drink
run	chew
swim	throw
jump	giggle
shout	sleep

Note: You may add ed to these words.

Adjectives
(describing words)

terrible	blue
wonderful	slimy
sleepy	smelly
silly	short
pretty	funny
loud	excited

What a _____ day this was! First I found

some _____ . But I had to _____

across a _____ to get to them. Then I had to

_____ through a _____ filled with

_____ . They made me feel _____ .

When that was done, I _____ with a rope across a

_____ . I could smell some _____ right

around the corner. I could hardly wait to _____ them!

After going through one more _____ , I was there!

At last, I could _____ and _____ some

_____ .

Carly the Coupon Clipper

Two-Digit Subtraction

Carly loves to clip coupons and save money by using them. Draw a line from the coupon to the product. Carly did not use one of her coupons. The first one has been done for you.

Price: 65¢
Carly paid: -30¢
 35¢

Price: 95¢
Carly paid: 45¢

15¢ off

Price: 50¢
Carly paid: 35¢

50¢ off

Price: 70¢
Carly paid: 60¢

10¢ off

Price: 75¢
Carly paid: 50¢

55¢ off

Prefix Pyramids

Prefixes

Artie the Archaeologist needs your help to rebuild some pyramids. Fill in each pyramid using words that begin with the prefix at the top. Use the words in the Word Box to help you build the words.

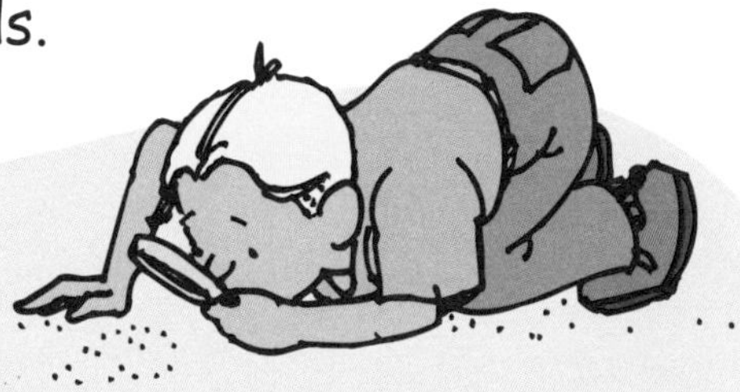

un-

unhappy

re-

mis-

WORD BOX

usual	treat	do	take	write
spell	pay	able	happy	

What Am I?

Count the syllables. Color.

1-syllable words **green**

2-syllable words **blue**

3-syllable words **red**

4-syllable words **yellow**

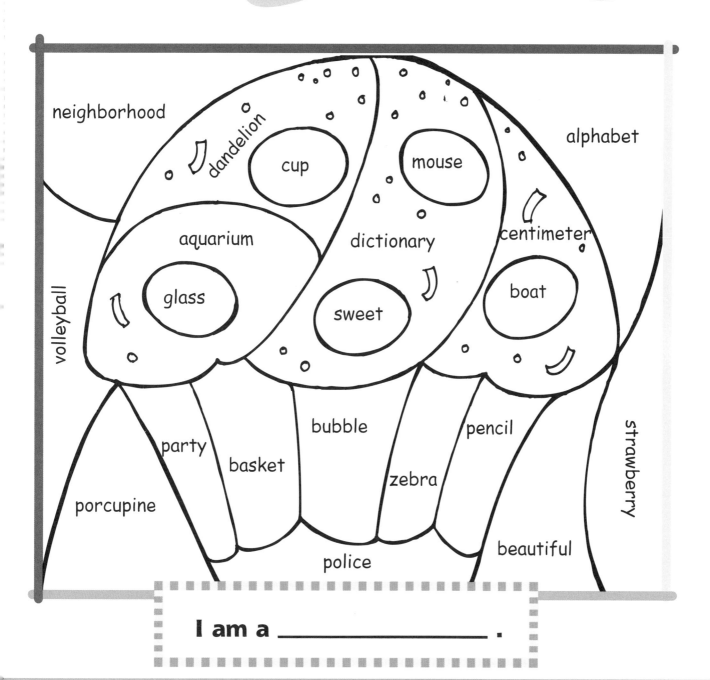

neighborhood

dandelion

cup

mouse

alphabet

aquarium

dictionary

centimeter

glass

sweet

boat

volleyball

party

basket

bubble

zebra

pencil

strawberry

porcupine

police

beautiful

I am a _____ **.**

113

Sum Time

Fill in the blocks with a number that will make each row across add up to 12. Then add down and write the sum of each column in the box.

114

In the Sea

There are so many things in the sea. But sometimes they are hard to find. Find and circle all the words in the Word Box.

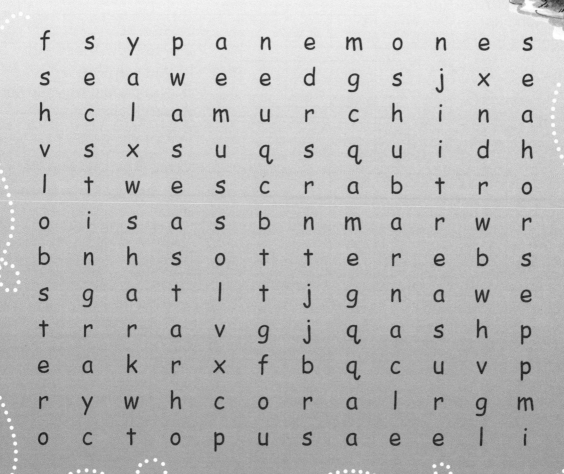

```
f  s  y  p  a  n  e  m  o  n  e  s
s  e  a  w  e  e  d  g  s  j  x  e
h  c  l  a  m  u  r  c  h  i  n  a
v  s  x  s  u  q  s  q  u  i  d  h
l  t  w  e  s  c  r  a  b  t  r  o
o  i  s  a  s  b  n  m  a  r  w  r
b  n  h  s  o  t  t  e  r  e  b  s
s  g  a  t  l  t  j  g  n  a  w  e
t  r  r  a  v  g  j  q  a  s  h  p
e  a  k  r  x  f  b  q  c  u  v  p
r  y  w  h  c  o  r  a  l  r  g  m
o  c  t  o  p  u  s  a  e  e  l  i
```

WORD BOX

anemone	eel	seaweed	treasure	barnacle	lobster
shark	urchin	clam	otter	squid	coral
octopus	sea star	crab	sea horse	stingray	

The Birthday Bash

This crossword puzzle is filled with birthday party words. Fill it in. Then unscramble the letters in the yellow squares to answer the riddle below.

Down
1. it's the main dish
3. it comes once a year
5. you play these, like Pin the Tail on the Donkey
6. it says "Happy Birthday!" and is hung up
7. he wears a big red nose

Across
2. you blow these out
4. you win this
5. the people at your party
8. you blow these up
9. you open these

WORD BOX

presents	games	guests	candles	prize
cake	banner	balloons	birthday	clown

What's the coolest part of the party? __ __ __ __ __ __ __ __

116

Gumball Game

Find the gumball needed to complete each problem.

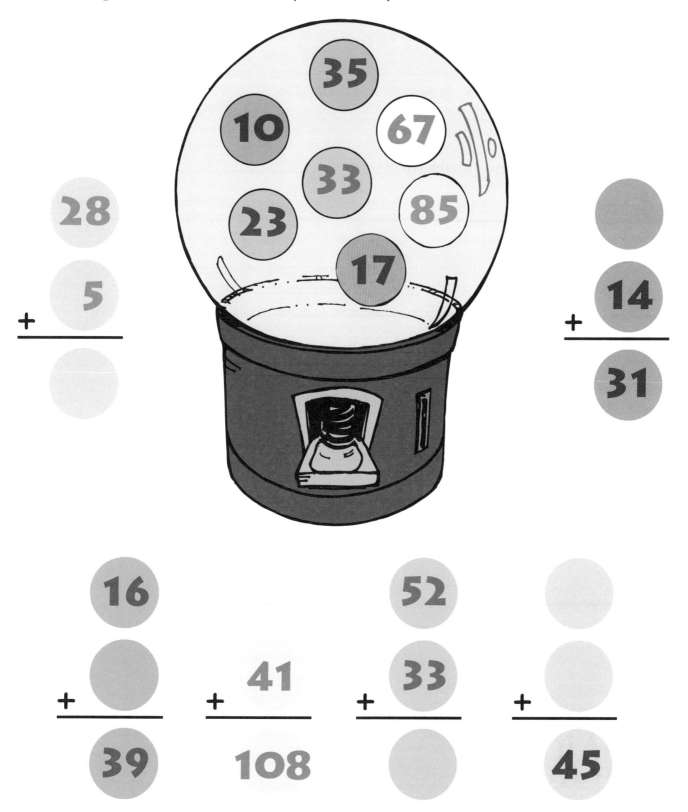

28
5
+ ___
___

14
+ ___
31

16
+ ___
39

41
+ ___
108

52
33
+ ___

+ ___
45

117

To the Finish Line!

These sentences are off to a good start, but they aren't finished. Finish each sentence in an interesting way.

The wild beast in the jungle suddenly _____

_____ .

One of these days, I'm going to _____

_____ .

Just as the game ended, _____

_____ .

As I opened the chest, I saw _____

_____ .

I can't believe he ate _____

_____ .

Dear Grandma

Jenny's birthday was last weekend. Her grandma from Florida sent her a big package of things. Unscramble the words to find out what Jenny got for her birthday. Draw a line to the picture that shows each word.

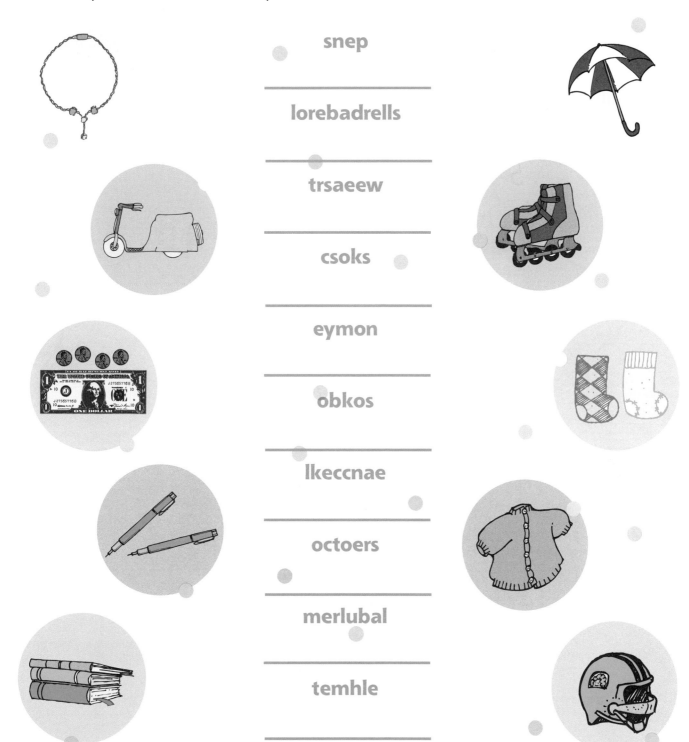

snep

_____

lorebadrells

_____

trsaeew

_____

csoks

_____

eymon

_____

obkos

_____

lkeccnae

_____

octoers

_____

merlubal

_____

temhle

_____

Webster's Super Spider Web

Webster and his friends love to add. They put numbers in each section of the web that add up to the number in the center. Help them finish each web.

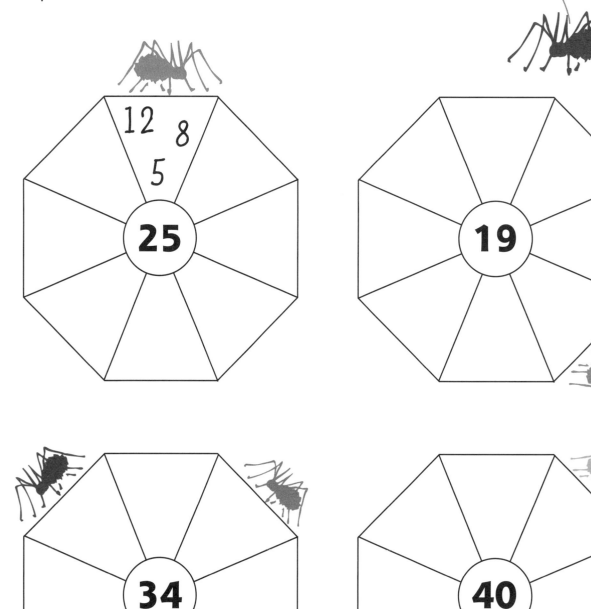

Put an End to It!

Each of the words in the Word Box has an ending, or suffix. Circle each suffix. Then use the words to complete the crossword puzzle.

Across
2. a special feeling between two people
6. not afraid
7. opposite of slowly

Down
1. a pipe cleaner is _____
3. wet weather
4. a machine to clean clothes
5. a kind of hint

WORD BOX

| quickly | bendable | washer | rainy |
| friendship | fearless | helpful | |

Muggsy's Messy Day

Read the story. Circle all of the adjectives, words that describe things. Can you find all 19?

Brady and Muggsy looked out the wet window. Fat drops of rain splashed outside. It was going to be a boring day. Brady watched two funny cartoons. Muggsy put his cold nose on Brady's hand. He looked at Brady with his big, sad eyes.

Brady knew Muggsy needed to go out. He opened the back door. Out went Muggsy! He jumped into muddy puddles. He rolled in dirty leaves. Then Muggsy found a smelly, old toy. He shook it until the wet stuffing was all over the soaked yard.

Brady grabbed a warm, dry towel. He called Muggsy. Soon Muggsy was clean, but Brady was dirty!

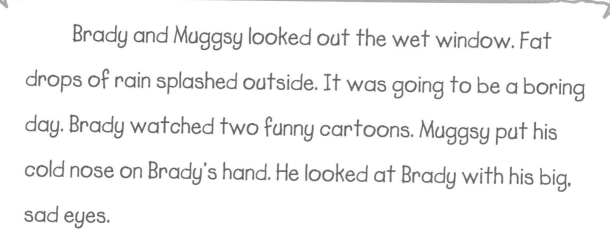

Three Little Squids

These three little squids have lots of arms. Each one has 10! Solve the squid problems below.

Each squid has 10 arms. How many in all?

10 + 10 + 10 = ☐   **OR**   3 squid x 10 arms = ☐

Each squid has 2 long arms. How many long arms in all?

2 + 2 + 2 = ☐   **OR**   3 squid x 2 long arms = ☐

Each squid has 3 blue arms. How many blue arms in all?

3 + 3 + 3 = ☐   **OR**   3 squid x 3 blue arms = ☐

Each squid has 5 purple arms. How many purple arms in all?

5 + 5 + 5 = ☐   **OR**   3 squid x 5 purple arms = ☐

★BONUS: Each squid has 8 short arms. How many short arms in all?

8 + 8 + 8 = ☐   **OR**   3 squid x 8 short arms = ☐

What's Hiding?

Something is hiding! You can find out what it is by knowing your nouns. Remember: A noun is a person, place, or thing.

Color proper nouns (ones that need a capital letter) orange.
Color all other nouns yellow.
Color all other words blue.

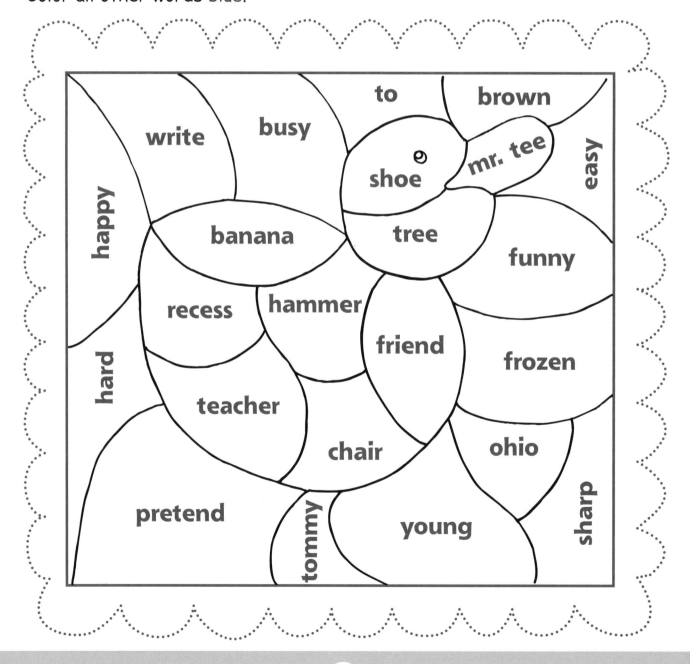

What Makes a Perfect Pet?

Tell what a perfect pet is like.

_____   _____

_____   _____

_____   _____

Now write a newspaper ad. Be sure to say what this pet will be like and include your name and phone number.

Wanted: A Perfect Pet

_____

_____

_____

_____

_____

_____

Big-Time Bowling

Addition

Max, Fred, and Jim are big-time bowlers. They are playing a very good team: Carl, Sam, and Don. Add up the scores to see which team won the tournament.

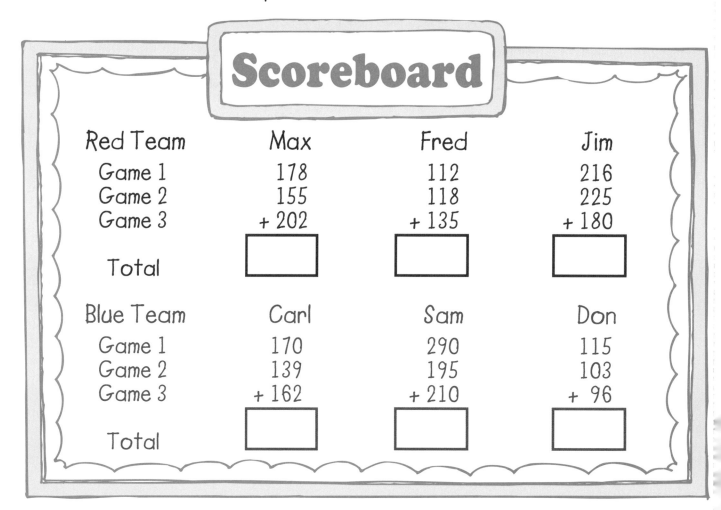

Scoreboard

Red Team	Max	Fred	Jim
Game 1	178	112	216
Game 2	155	118	225
Game 3	+ 202	+ 135	+ 180
Total			

Blue Team	Carl	Sam	Don
Game 1	170	290	115
Game 2	139	195	103
Game 3	+ 162	+ 210	+ 96
Total			

Now add these:

Max's total _____   Carl's total _____

Fred's total _____   Sam's total _____

Jim's total _____   Don's total _____

Red Team's Total _____   Blue Team's Total _____

Who won the tournament? _____

Buy My Stuff

Here's an ad for some yummy pies.

Now it's your turn! Here are some products that need an ad. Choose a product and write an ad for it in the box below. Draw pictures to make your ad more interesting.

- Roller Skates
- Magic Show
- Homemade Ice Cream
- Face Painting

Chicken Little Tries Again

Chicken Little is so worried about the sky falling that he doesn't know which verb to use. Can you help? Write the correct verb in each blank.

For a long time I _____ to tell everyone that the sky
  try   tried

_____ falling. But they _____ not believe me. They
  was   is   did   does

just _____ at me.
  laugh   laughed

This morning when I _____ out of bed, it _____
                      got   get   happens   happened

again. Out of nowhere _____ a big piece of the sky. It
                         fall   fell

_____ me on the head with a clunk! But this time I
  hitted   hit

_____ ready. Before I _____ outside, I
  was   were   walk   walked

_____ something. I _____ on my brand new
  does   did   put   putted

helmet. Now no one _____ at me. But they might
                      will laugh   laughed

_____ to _____ a helmet like mine!
  want   wants   buys   buy

Which Shelf, Elf?

Ordinal Numbers, Reasoning

Eddie the Elf is looking for a book. Find out which book he wants by following the clues below. Count from top to bottom—the first shelf is on the top. Make an X through each shelf that the book is **not** on.

1. It is not on the top shelf.

2. It is between the first shelf and the fifth shelf.

3. It is not on the third shelf.

4. Two shelves are left. It is on the upper one.

5. Counting from the left, the book is not the first book.

6. It is not the third or the sixth book.

7. It is the odd-numbered one.

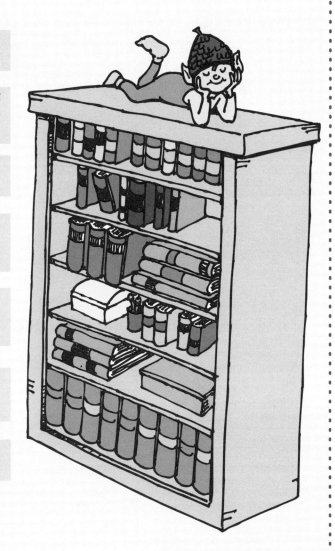

Answer:

Eddie Elf's book is on the _____ shelf.

It is the _____ book from the left.

The color of the book is _____ .

Answer Key

Checking your child's work is an important part of learning. It allows you to see what your child knows well and what areas need more practice. It also provides an opportunity for you to help your child understand that making mistakes is a part of learning.

When an error is discovered, ask your child to look carefully at the question or problem. Errors often occur through misreading. Your child can quickly correct these errors. Help your child with items she or he finds difficult.

Page 4

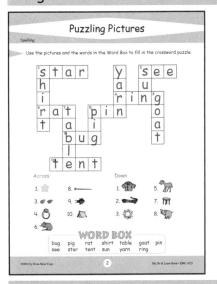

Page 5

Page 6

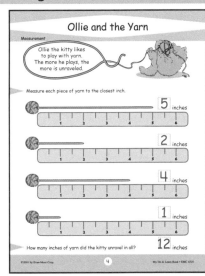

Page 7

Page 8

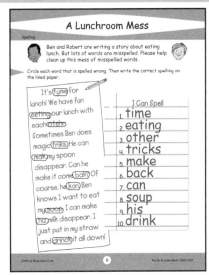

Page 9

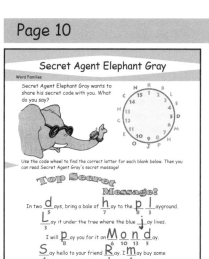

Secret Agent Elephant Gray

Word Families

Secret Agent Elephant Gray wants to share his secret code with you. What do you say?

Use the code wheel to find the correct letter for each blank below. Then you can read Secret Agent Gray's secret message!

Top Secret Message!

In two **d**ays, bring a bale of **h**ay to the **pl**ayground.
Lay it under the tree where the blue **j**ay lives.
I will **p**ay you for it on **Mond**ay.
Say hello to your friend **R**ay. I **m**ay buy some
hay from him **somed**ay, too.
E. **Gr**ay

Flower Power!

Short and Long Vowels

What a pretty patch of posies!
But they need some color to make them even prettier. You can help!

Read the word in each flower. If the word has a long vowel sound, color that flower purple. If the word has a short vowel sound, color that flower yellow.

tune • see • get • mop
thin • fun • pine
cap • toad • sweet

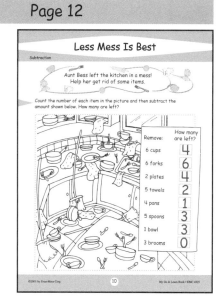

Less Mess Is Best

Subtraction

Aunt Bess left the kitchen in a mess! Help her get rid of some items.

Count the number of each item in the picture and then subtract the amount shown below. How many are left?

Remove:	How many are left?
6 cups	4
6 forks	6
2 plates	4
5 towels	2
4 pans	1
5 spoons	3
1 bowl	0
3 brooms	0

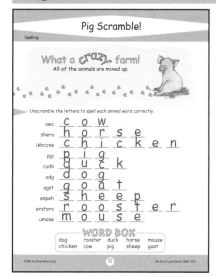

Pig Scramble!

Spelling

What a crazy farm!
All of the animals are mixed up.

Unscramble the letters to spell each animal word correctly.

owc — **cow**
shero — **horse**
ikhccne — **chicken**
pgi — **pig**
cudk — **duck**
odg — **dog**
agot — **goat**
espeh — **sheep**
erstoro — **rooster**
umose — **mouse**

WORD BOX
dog   rooster   duck   horse   mouse
chicken   cow   pig   sheep   goat

Make the Connection

Alphabetical Order

Connect the dots in alphabetical order. Then fill in the blanks below to tell what the picture is.

cap • dust • eggs • flower • boat • grass • alligator • hat • zipper • kiss • yarn • jungle • lion • mask • x-ray • island • water • neighbor • valley • umbrella • onion • poppy • tulip • queen • storm • roses

Unscramble these letters:
tewagrni anc
watering can

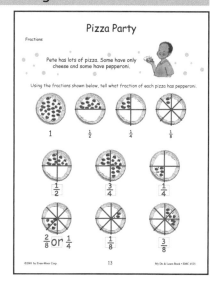

Pizza Party

Fractions

Pete has lots of pizza. Some have only cheese and some have pepperoni.

Using the fractions shown below, tell what fraction of each pizza is pepperoni.

1   $\frac{1}{2}$ $\frac{1}{4}$ $\frac{1}{8}$

$\frac{1}{2}$ $\frac{3}{4}$ $\frac{1}{4}$

$\frac{2}{8}$ or $\frac{1}{4}$ $\frac{1}{8}$ $\frac{3}{8}$

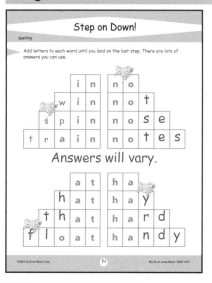

Step on Down!

Spelling

Add letters to each word until you land on the last step. There are lots of answers you can use.

i n   n o
w i n   n o t
s p i n   n o s e
t r a i n   n o t e s

Answers will vary.

a t   h a
h a t   h a y
t h a t   h a r d
f l o a t   h a n d y

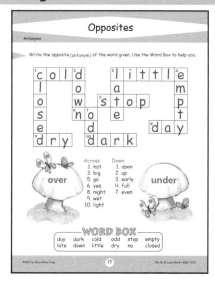

Opposites

Antonyms

Write the opposite (antonym) of the word given. Use the Word Box to help you.

cold • little • empty • lose • stop • now • day • dry • dark

over   under

Across
1. hot
3. big
5. go
6. yes
8. night
9. wet
10. light

Down
1. open
2. up
3. early
4. full
7. even

WORD BOX
day   dark   cold   odd   stop   empty
late   down   little   dry   no   closed

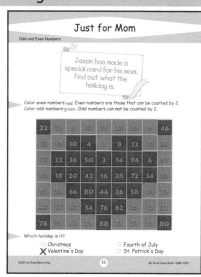

Just for Mom

Odd and Even Numbers

Jason has made a special card for his mom. Find out what the holiday is.

Color even numbers red. Even numbers are those that can be counted by 2. Color odd numbers green. Odd numbers can not be counted by 2.

22	71	91	39	27	85	9	46
35	99	10	4	7	8	12	95
23	22	36	50	2	14	94	97
61	18	20	42	16	28	72	34
51	38	66	80	44	26	58	31
47	11	67	34	76	62	16	79
78	17	36	29	88	57	51	80

Which holiday is it?
○ Christmas   ○ Fourth of July
✗ Valentine's Day   ○ St. Patrick's Day

Brand New Nursery Rhymes
Creative Thinking

Add your own words to make these old nursery rhymes new.

Jack and Jill went up the _____   **Answers**
To get a _____ of _____   **will vary.**

Mary had a little _____. Its _____ was
_____ as _____

Little Boy _____ come blow your _____,
The _____ is in the _____.

Little Miss _____ sat on a _____
Eating her _____ and _____.

Draw a picture of one of the new rhymes.

Pictures will vary.

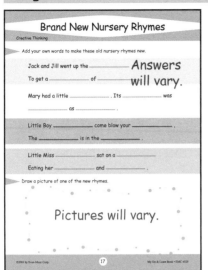

Twelve Months of Missing Vowels
Spelling

Someone tried to take the vowels from the months of the year!

Put them back where they belong.

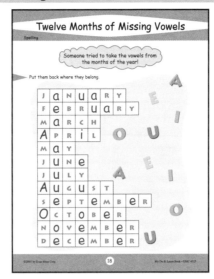

Leon's Lemonade Stand
Money

Leon doesn't have a price for his lemonade. He lets the customers pay him whatever they want.

Count the money and write how much each customer gave him.

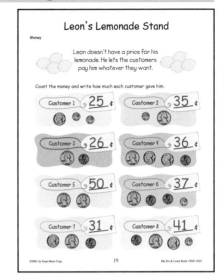

Customer 1 — 25¢   Customer 2 — 35¢
Customer 3 — 26¢   Customer 4 — 36¢
Customer 5 — 50¢   Customer 6 — 37¢
Customer 7 — 31¢   Customer 8 — 41¢

Choo-choo! Choo-choo!
Sound Words

Listen to the train. It is carrying lots of sound words (like choo-choo!). Can you complete the words?

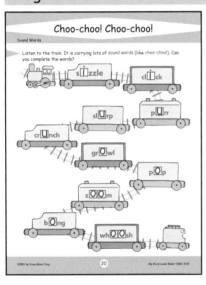

sizzle, click, slurp, purr, crunch, growl, pop, zoom, bong, whoosh

Tock! Tick! The Clock is Sick!
Word Families

Poor sick clock! Its tick won't tock.
But it will feel better as soon as you solve the puzzle below.

All of the words belong to the -ick or the -ock families. Fill in the blanks with the correct letters.

dogs do this — lick
thin piece of wood — stick
you do this to a football — kick
a stone — rock
this helps to keep things safe — lock
a bunch of sheep — flock
a baby hen — chick
on your foot — sock
a bug — tick
_____ or treat — trick

Diamond Drop
Number Order

Darice dropped her diamonds! Help her put them back in order. Do each row separately. The first one has been done for you.

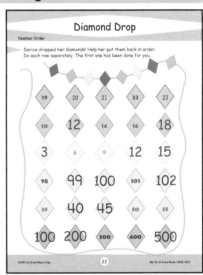

19 20 21 22 23
10 12 14 16 18
3 6 9 12 15
98 99 100 101 102
35 40 45 50 55
100 200 300 400 500

Make It Rhyme
Word Family

Fill in the blanks with -ail words to make a rhyme. Then draw a picture to show what happened.

Fido knocked over the **pail**
When he barked and wagged his **tail**.

Pictures will vary.

She waited and waited for the **mail**.
It must have been delivered by a **snail**.

Five chicks and Mother **quail**
Hiked along the forest **trail**.

What's in the Cupboard?
Compound Words

Look at all the goodies in the box. Each one is a compound word (a word made of two words put together). Use a word from each list to name each thing in the cupboard.

sea
sun
note
air
cow
dragon
tea
candle

book
pot
stick
fly
boy
plane
flower
shell

seashell
sunflower
notebook
airplane
cowboy
dragonfly
teapot
candlestick

Count the Cards
Place Value

Bobby and his friends have a huge baseball card collection. They want to count every single card. Show how many cards each person has.

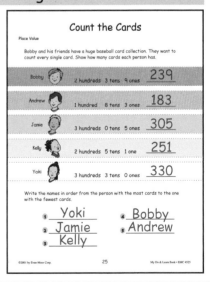

Bobby	2 hundreds 3 tens 9 ones	239
Andrew	1 hundred 8 tens 3 ones	183
Jamie	3 hundreds 0 tens 5 ones	305
Kelly	2 hundreds 5 tens 1 one	251
Yoki	3 hundreds 3 tens 0 ones	330

Write the names in order from the person with the most cards to the one with the fewest cards.

1. Yoki
2. Jamie
3. Kelly
4. Bobby
5. Andrew

Page 28

What's Here?
Long and Short Vowels

Find out what is hidden in the picture.
Color the words with short vowels yellow.
Color the words with long vowels blue.

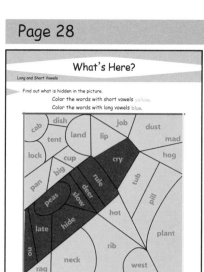

What did you find? **a crayon**

Page 29

Happy Endings
Plurals

Each of these pictures shows one thing.
But what if there were two?
How would you write the plural word?

Add s to most words to make them plural. But add es to words that end in ch, sh, s, or x.

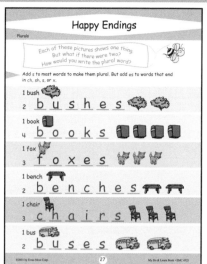

1 bush
2 **b u s h e s**

1 book
4 **b o o k s**

1 fox
3 **f o x e s**

1 bench
2 **b e n c h e s**

1 chair
3 **c h a i r s**

1 bus
2 **b u s e s**

Page 30

T-Shirt Trouble
Patterns

Coach Smith has a big problem!
Some of the team T-shirts are missing their numbers. But he has a good idea. He put the shirts in order. Now he can see which numbers are missing.

Can you figure out what number belongs on each shirt?

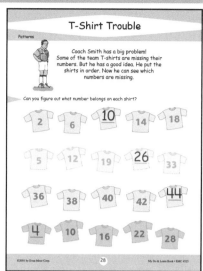

Page 31

Pow! Bang! Kerplop!
Sound Words

Unscramble these words to see what sound they make. Draw a string from the balloon to the correct sound word below.

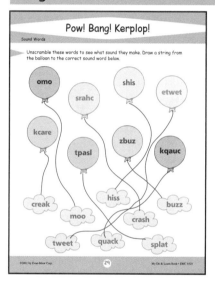

Page 32

We'll Go Fishing
Contractions

Uncle Roger wants to take you fishing! He has a special pole for each fish.

Match each pole with the contraction it belongs to. The first one has been done for you.

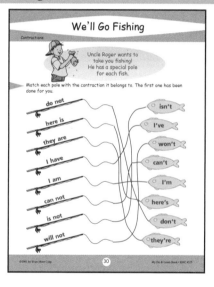

Page 33

Dot 2 Dot
Counting by 2s

Follow the dots, counting by 2, until the picture below is through!

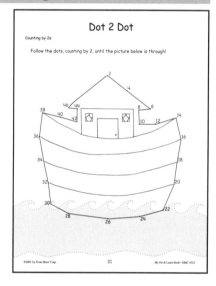

Page 34

What Animal Are You Like?
Creative Writing

Compare yourself with an animal. Tell how you are like that animal and in what ways you are different.

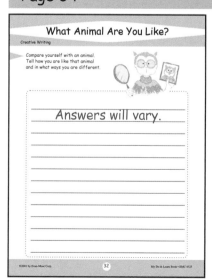

Answers will vary.

Page 35

Nine Fine Fill-ins
Word Families

Fill in the crossword puzzle using the -in and -ine words in the Word Box.

Across
2. skinny
4. thin rope
5. backbone
7. bottom of a face
9. glow

Down
1. 4 + 5 =
3. a look alike
6. Christmas trees
8. not to lose

WORD BOX
pines chin nine thin
shine spine win twine

Page 36

A Penny Saved
Place Value

Kevin, Ahmed, and Melissa are all saving pennies. They have stacked them in sets of 10.

How many pennies does each person have?

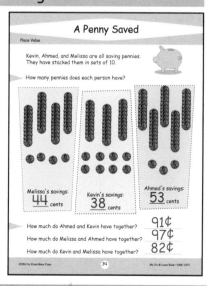

Melissa's savings: **44** cents
Kevin's savings: **38** cents
Ahmed's savings: **53** cents

How much do Ahmed and Kevin have together? **91¢**
How much do Melissa and Ahmed have together? **97¢**
How much do Kevin and Melissa have together? **82¢**

The Spelling Well

Spelling

Jack and Jill have made a spill.

Their pail of words from the spelling well have all poured out.

Circle the words that are spelled correctly. Make an X through the misspelled words. Then write them correctly on the lines.

said
turtle
forty
grade

nurse
girl
shirt
twenty

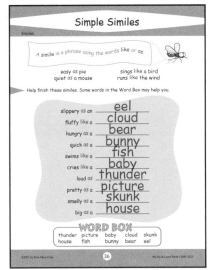

Simple Similes

Similes

A simile is a phrase using the words *like* or *as*

easy as pie
quiet as a mouse
sings like a bird
runs like the wind

Help finish these similes. Some words in the Word Box may help you.

slippery as an **eel**
fluffy like a **cloud**
hungry as a **bear**
quick as a **bunny**
swims like a **fish**
cries like a **baby**
loud as **thunder**
pretty as a **picture**
smelly as a **skunk**
big as a **house**

WORD BOX
thunder picture baby cloud skunk
house fish bunny bear eel

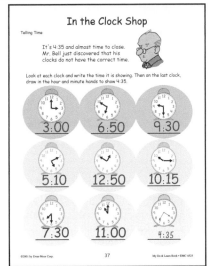

In the Clock Shop

Telling Time

It's 4:35 and almost time to close. Mr. Bell just discovered that his clocks do not have the correct time.

Look at each clock and write the time it is showing. Then on the last clock, draw in the hour and minute hands to show 4:35.

3:00   6:50   9:30
5:10   12:50   10:15
7:30   11:00   4:35

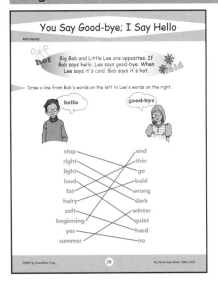

You Say Good-bye; I Say Hello

Antonyms

Big Bob and Little Lee are opposites. If Bob says hello, Lee says good-bye. When Lee says it's cold, Bob says it's hot.

Draw a line from Bob's words on the left to Lee's words on the right.

hello   good-bye

stop   end
right   thin
light   go
loud   bald
fat   wrong
hairy   dark
soft   winter
beginning   quiet
yes   hard
summer   no

Short and Sweet

Abbreviations

Some words can be written in a shorter way. These are called abbreviations.

Fill in the crossword puzzle below using the complete word for each abbreviation.

December
quart
inch
street

Across
2. Dec.
5. qt.
6. in.
7. St.

Down
1. Mr.
2. Dr.
3. cm
4. Rd.

WORD BOX
centimeter Street inch Mister
quart Doctor Road December

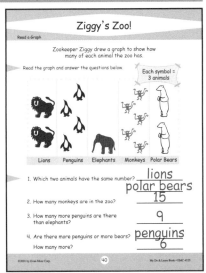

Ziggy's Zoo!

Read a Graph

Zookeeper Ziggy drew a graph to show how many of each animal the zoo has.

Read the graph and answer the questions below.

Each symbol = 3 animals

Lions Penguins Elephants Monkeys Polar Bears

1. Which two animals have the same number? **lions polar bears**

2. How many monkeys are in the zoo? **15**

3. How many more penguins are there than elephants? **9**

4. Are there more penguins or more bears? **penguins**
How many more? **6**

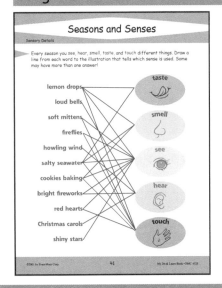

Seasons and Senses

Sensory Details

Every season you see, hear, smell, taste, and touch different things. Draw a line from each word to the illustration that tells which sense is used. Some may have more than one answer!

lemon drops
loud bells
soft mittens
fireflies
howling wind
salty seawater
cookies baking
bright fireworks
red hearts
Christmas carols
shiny stars

taste
smell
see
hear
touch

Drew's Dream

/dr/ Blend

Drew is dreaming of things that begin with the letters *dr*. Fill in the missing words to tell about Drew's dream.

Drew dreamed that he sat up in bed. He had heard a noise. The bottom **drawer** of his **dresser** was opening. Noises were coming from inside it.

Suddenly the strangest parade you ever saw marched out of the drawer. Leading the parade was a clown wearing a lacy **dress**. As he marched, he waved a **drill** to keep the beat. Next to come was a centipede beating a **drum** with his many feet. A funny puppy with short, little legs and long, **droopy** ears was third in the parade. Finally, there was a colorful **dragonfly drinking** soda as he **drove** a race car.

The next morning, Drew vowed to never eat chocolate and a pickle before going to bed!

WORD BOX
drill droopy drove dress dresser
drawer dragonfly drum drinking

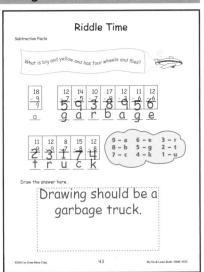

Riddle Time

Subtraction Facts

What is big and yellow and has four wheels and flies?

18	12	14	10	17	11	12
-9	-7	-5	-7	-3	-4	-6
9	5	9	3	8	9	5 6
a	g	a	r	b	a	g e

11	12	8	15	12
2	3	1	7	4
t	r	u	c k

9 – a   6 – e   3 – r
8 – b   5 – g   2 – t
7 – c   4 – k   1 – u

Draw the answer here.

Drawing should be a garbage truck.

Page 46

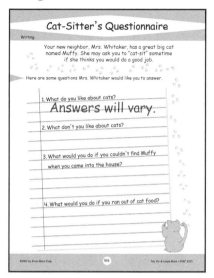

Cat-Sitter's Questionnaire

Writing

Your new neighbor, Mrs. Whitaker, has a great big cat named Muffy. She may ask you to "cat-sit" sometime if she thinks you would do a good job.

Here are some questions Mrs. Whitaker would like you to answer.

1. What do you like about cats?

Answers will vary.

2. What don't you like about cats?

3. What would you do if you couldn't find Muffy when you came into the house?

4. What would you do if you ran out of cat food?

Page 47

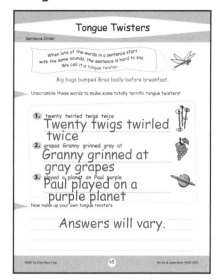

Tongue Twisters

Sentence Order

When lots of the words in a sentence start with the same sounds, the sentence is hard to say. We call it a tongue twister.

Big bugs bumped Brad badly before breakfast.

Unscramble these words to make some totally terrific tongue twisters!

1. twenty twirled twigs twice
Twenty twigs twirled twice

2. grapes Granny grinned gray at
Granny grinned at gray grapes

3. played a planet on Paul purple
Paul played on a purple planet

Now make up your own tongue twisters.

Answers will vary.

Page 48

Strike Out the Numbers!

Number Patterns

Make an X through the number that does not belong in each set below. Then write the correct number. The first one has been done for you.

Correct Number

4	5	6	X	8	9	**7**
10	15	20	25	30	37	40	**35**
3	6	9	12	15	19	**18**
$1.00	$1.25	$1.50	$1.75	$2.25	**$2.00**
12	16	18	20	22	24	**14**
200	350	400	450	500	**300**

Page 49

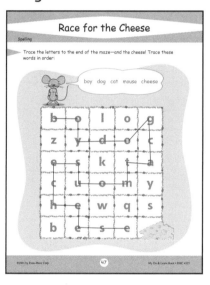

Race for the Cheese

Spelling

Trace the letters to the end of the maze—and the cheese! Trace these words in order:

boy dog cat mouse cheese

Page 50

Farmer Sam's BIG Trouble

Word Families

What can Farmer Sam do? Something is eating his turnips!

Solve the puzzle and you will find the answer.

fire	f l a m e
lives in a shell	c l a m
not wild	t a m e
eggs and _____	h a m
what you call yourself	n a m e
sweet potato	y a m
like jelly	j a m
closing a door hard	s l a m
something to play	g a m e
picture _____	f r a m e

WORD BOX
slam   game   ham   tame   name
jam   flame   frame   yam   clam

Now write each of the letters with a number on the matching lines below. Then you will have an answer for Farmer Sam.

Tell the r a m to s c r a m !
1 2 3   4 5 1 2 3

Page 51

I Love Cookies!

Money

Circle how much money I need to buy these cookies.

Answers will vary.

10¢ 5¢

I spent 35¢. How many cookies did I buy?
3

1

Page 52

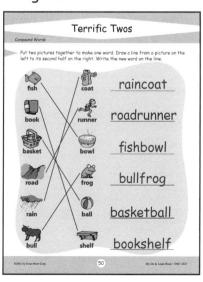

Terrific Twos

Compound Words

Put two pictures together to make one word. Draw a line from a picture on the left to its second half on the right. Write the new word on the line.

fish — coat
book — runner
basket — bowl
road — frog
rain — ball
bull — shelf

raincoat
roadrunner
fishbowl
bullfrog
basketball
bookshelf

Page 53

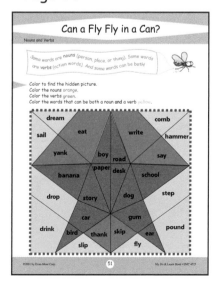

Can a Fly Fly in a Can?

Nouns and Verbs

Some words are nouns (person, place, or thing). Some words are verbs (action words). And some words can be both!

Color to find the hidden picture.
Color the nouns orange.
Color the verbs green.
Color the words that can be both a noun and a verb yellow.

dream   comb
sail   eat   write   hammer
yank   boy   road   say
paper   desk
banana   school
drop   story   dog   step
car   gum
drink   bird   thank   skip   ear   pound
slip   fly

Page 54

Secret Message

Column Addition

Solve the problems to answer this riddle.

What do you call a cat that loves lemons?

s	r	u	a	u
11	10	9	8	14
10	12	8	5	16
8	9	9	3	3
+ 6	+ 9	+ 12	+ 7	+ 4
35	31	37	29	37

p	s	o	s
11	7	12	10
9	8	10	7
10	15	9	5
+ 9	+ 5	+ 2	+ 13
39	35	33	35

a   s o u r   p u s s
29   35 33 37 31   39 37 35 35

Shhhhhh! She's Sleeping!
/sh/, /sk/, and /sl/ Blends

Sheri is dreaming about many things.

Fill in the puzzle with the sh, sk, and sl words from her dream.

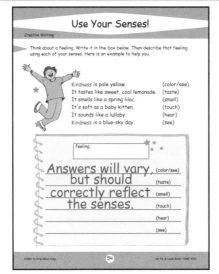

Use Your Senses!
Creative Writing

Think about a feeling. Write it in the box below. Then describe that feeling using each of your senses. Here is an example to help you.

Kindness is pale yellow. (color/see)
It tastes like sweet, cool lemonade. (taste)
It smells like a spring lilac. (smell)
It's soft as a baby kitten. (touch)
It sounds like a lullaby. (hear)
Kindness is a blue-sky day. (see)

feeling:

Answers will vary, (color/see)
but should (taste)
correctly reflect (smell)
the senses. (touch)
_____ (hear)
_____ (see)

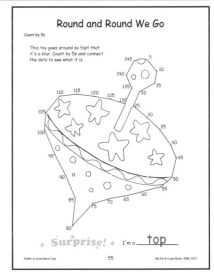

Round and Round We Go
Count by 5s

This toy goes around so fast that it's a blur. Count by 5s and connect the dots to see what it is.

Surprise! I'm a ___top___

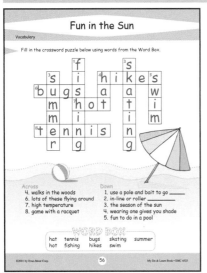

Fun in the Sun
Vocabulary

Fill in the crossword puzzle below using words from the Word Box.

Across
4. walks in the woods
6. lots of these flying around
7. high temperature
8. game with a racquet

Down
1. use a pole and bait to go _____
2. in-line or roller _____
3. the season of the sun
4. wearing one gives you shade
5. fun to do in a pool

WORD BOX
hat | tennis | bugs | skating | summer
hot | fishing | hikes | swim

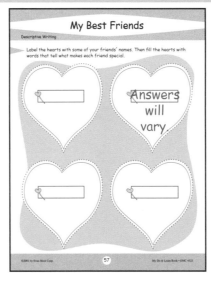

My Best Friends
Descriptive Writing

Label the hearts with some of your friends' names. Then fill the hearts with words that tell what makes each friend special.

Answers will vary

What Time Is It?
Time

All of Wayne's watches have stopped. Use the digital clocks to help him set the hands in the correct places.

8:45
3:20
12:15
6:05

Which time is Wayne's lunchtime? 12:15
Which time is Wayne's bedtime? 8:45

It's a Snap!
Long and Short a

Put on your thinking cap and help the ape get this crossword puzzle in shape. All the answers will have a short a or a long a.

Across
1. Superman wears a _____
3. _____ are a fruit
5. a circle is a _____
7. an afternoon rest

Down
1. a baseball hat
2. used to catch something
4. to hit
6. a big monkey

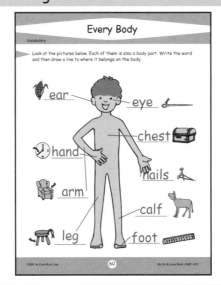

Every Body
Vocabulary

Look at the pictures below. Each of them is also a body part. Write the word and then draw a line to where it belongs on the body.

ear
eye
chest
hand
nails
arm
calf
leg
foot

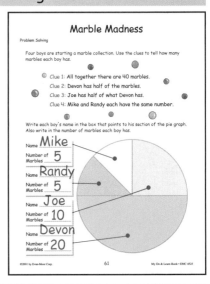

Marble Madness
Problem Solving

Four boys are starting a marble collection. Use the clues to tell how many marbles each boy has.

Clue 1: All together there are 40 marbles.
Clue 2: Devon has half of the marbles.
Clue 3: Joe has half of what Devon has.
Clue 4: Mike and Randy each have the same number.

Write each boy's name in the box that points to his section of the pie graph. Also write in the number of marbles each boy has.

Name Mike
Number of Marbles 5

Name Randy
Number of Marbles 5

Name Joe
Number of Marbles 10

Name Devon
Number of Marbles 20

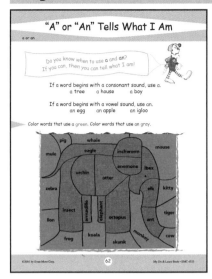

"A" or "An" Tells What I Am

a or an

Do you know when to use *a* and *an*? If you can, then you can tell what I am!

If a word begins with a consonant sound, use *a*.
a tree   a house   a boy

If a word begins with a vowel sound, use *an*.
an egg   an apple   an igloo

Color words that use *a* green. Color words that use *an* gray.

pig whale mouse
mule eagle inchworm
urchin anemone ibex
zebra otter elk kitty
insect armadillo elephant tiger
lion octopus ant
frog koala skunk monkey cow

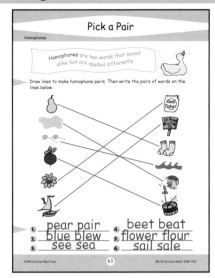

Pick a Pair

Homophones

Homophones are two words that sound alike but are spelled differently.

Draw lines to make homophone pairs. Then write the pairs of words on the lines below.

1. pear pair
2. blue blew
3. see sea
4. beet beat
5. flower flour
6. sail sale

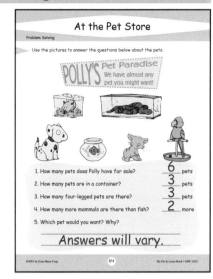

At the Pet Store

Problem Solving

Use the pictures to answer the questions below about the pets.

POLLY'S Pet Paradise
We have almost any pet you might want!

1. How many pets does Polly have for sale? 6 pets
2. How many pets are in a container? 3 pets
3. How many four-legged pets are there? 3 pets
4. How many more mammals are there than fish? 2 more
5. Which pet would you want? Why?

Answers will vary.

Here Kitty, Kitty, Kitty!

Visual Discrimination

Cats love to hide—under the couch, up in a tree, or in a closet. Can you find all of the cat words hiding in the puzzle below? Use the Word Box to help you find all 12 words.

WORD BOX
kitten claws meow whiskers tiger lion
cougar roar purr wildcat scratch litter

Aunt Abby's Attic Alphabet

Creative Thinking

Aunt Abby has some unusual things in her attic. What do you think she found?

Write at least one thing for each letter of the alphabet.

a ___ n ___
b ___ o ___
c ___ Answers will vary but should match each letter.
d ___ p ___
e ___ r ___
f ___ s ___
g ___ t ___
h ___ u ___
i ___ v ___
j ___ w ___
k ___ x ___
l ___ y ___
m ___ z ___

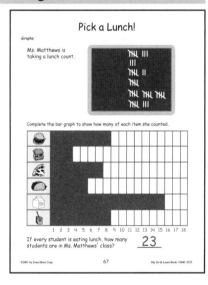

Pick a Lunch!

Graphs

Ms. Matthews is taking a lunch count.

Complete the bar graph to show how many of each item she counted.

1 2 3 4 5 6 7 8 9 10 11 12 13 14 15 16 17 18

If every student is eating lunch, how many students are in Ms. Matthews' class? 23

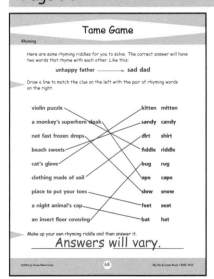

Tame Game

Rhyming

Here are some rhyming riddles for you to solve. The correct answer will have two words that rhyme with each other. Like this:

unhappy father ⟶ sad dad

Draw a line to match the clue on the left with the pair of rhyming words on the right.

violin puzzle   kitten mitten
a monkey's superhero cloak   sandy candy
not fast frozen drops   dirt shirt
beach sweets   fiddle riddle
cat's glove   bug rug
clothing made of soil   ape cape
place to put your toes   slow snow
a night animal's cap   feet seat
an insect floor covering   bat hat

Make up your own rhyming riddle and then answer it.

Answers will vary.

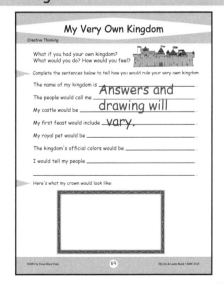

My Very Own Kingdom

Creative Thinking

What if you had your own kingdom? What would you do? How would you feel?

Complete the sentences below to tell how you would rule your very own kingdom

The name of my kingdom is ___
The people would call me ___
My castle would be ___   Answers and drawing will vary.
My first feast would include ___
My royal pet would be ___
The kingdom's official colors would be ___
I would tell my people ___

Here's what my crown would look like:

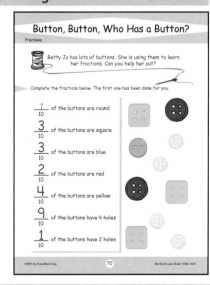

Button, Button, Who Has a Button?

Fractions

Betty Jo has lots of buttons. She is using them to learn her fractions. Can you help her out?

Complete the fractions below. The first one has been done for you.

$\frac{7}{10}$ of the buttons are round
$\frac{3}{10}$ of the buttons are square
$\frac{3}{10}$ of the buttons are blue
$\frac{2}{10}$ of the buttons are red
$\frac{4}{10}$ of the buttons are yellow
$\frac{9}{10}$ of the buttons have 4 holes
$\frac{1}{10}$ of the buttons have 2 holes

Puzzling Palindromes
Palindromes

A palindrome is a word that is spelled the same backward as it is forward.

Find and circle 26 palindromes in the story below. Some are used more than once. The first one has been done for you.

peep! ← → peep!

One day (Bob) and (Anna) went to the mountains. Their (dad) drove until (noon). He got tired, so they stopped to buy some (pop) to drink. (Mom) waited and waited for (Dad) to come back to the car. (Toot) the horn," said (Bob). So she (did).

"I'm coming!" called (Dad). He gave the (pop) to (Mom).

"I think we're lost," said (Anna). She was just playing a (gag) on (Dad).

"Just keep your (eye) on the map," said (Mom). "We'll be fine. (Anna) (sees) where we're going."

Soon they were at the river. They rode in a (kayak).

"Let's have some fun!" said (Dad).

And (Bob), (Anna), (Mom), and (Dad) (did)!

71

Do You Want a Bat or a Bat?
Homophones

Some words look alike but mean different things.

bat   bat

Look at the definitions on each side. Then write the word that is the same in the middle. The first one has been done for you.

group of musicians	band	thin rubber strip
beak of a bird	bill	paper that tells what is owed
did see	saw	cutting tool
finger jewelry	ring	bell sound
three feet	yard	area around a building
go together	match	stick that makes fire
inside of hand	palm	kind of a tree
enclosed area	pen	a writing object

WORD BOX
yard bill palm pen saw ring match

72

Count the Shapes
Geometric Shapes

Match.

circle
rectangle
triangle
square

How many squares? 7   How many triangles? 5

How many rectangles? 7   How many circles? 7

73

Match the Action
Synonyms

Draw a line to match the action words (verbs) with their synonyms (words that mean the same).

run   drag
draw   giggle
talk   purchase
laugh   leap
yell   tremble
jump   chat
pull   sob
eat   shout
cry   capture
catch   sketch
buy   gallop
shake   nibble

Can you run as fast as a horse can gallop?

74

I Won't Do It!
Contractions

Change the underlined words in the story to contractions. Use the contractions in the Word Box. The first one has been done for you.

Lisa is not happy. Today is her dance recital. She is upset! Maybe Lisa is just nervous. She told her mom that she will not dance. "I am not going to do it!" said Lisa. "And you cannot make me."

"We will see," said her mom. Soon they drove off. "Let us just think about all the fun you have had," she told Lisa. "That is the thing to do."

Soon Lisa was at the recital. "I have had fun dancing," Lisa thought. "Maybe I will give it a try." And she did.

"You are a good dancer," everyone told Lisa. "What is your secret?"

"I cannot tell you," she answered. Then she smiled.

isn't,
She's
won't
I'm
can't,
We'll
Let's
you've
That's
I've
I'll
You're
What's
can't

WORD BOX
I'll   you're won't let's you've that's isn't
can't   she's   I've   what's I'm   we'll

75

Yard Sale Today!
Addition

Lena, Bill, Mark, and Sally are going to the Big City Summer Yard Sale.

Look at all of the items for sale. Tell how much each person spent.

Receipt

Lena bought the kangaroo toy and candle.
She spent 90 ¢.

Bill bought the baseball and pencil.
He spent 75 ¢.

Mark bought the hat and comic book.
He spent 95 ¢.

Sally bought the bank and mitten.
She spent 90 ¢.

10¢ 30¢ 45¢ 35¢ 75¢ 15¢ 55¢ 85¢

Who spent the most money? Mark
Which two people spent the same amount? Lena and Sally

76

Recipe for a Sandwich
Creative Writing

Create a new, yummy sandwich. Draw a diagram to show its layers. Then write a recipe for all those who would like to try it out.

My Sandwich

diagram:

I named it: _____

You will need: _____   _____

Here's how to make it:
Answers and drawing will vary.

77

Words on the Move
Verbs

wiggle   flutter
wobble   twist gallop strut

Some verbs aren't for standing still. With your body, show what the words above mean. Then find other verbs for moving. Make a list of them here.

_____   _____
Answers will vary.
_____   _____

Use some of your moving words to describe an animal.
_____
_____

With a twist of her body, the cat wiggled out of my arms and leaped away.

78

Riddle Time
Two-Digit Addition and Subtraction

The more we dry, the wetter we get.

93 t   56 w   61 b   90 s   77 a
80 h   26 o   70 e   38 l

Add or subtract. Write the letter that goes with each answer.

22	86	37	52		48	93	84	55	70	87
+39	− 9	+56	+28		+45	−67	−28	+15	−32	+ 3
61	77	93	80		93	26	56	70	38	90
b	a	t	h		t	o	w	e	l	s

79

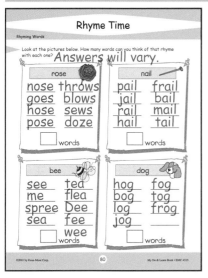

Rhyme Time

Rhyming Words

Look at the pictures below. How many words can you think of that rhyme with each one? Answers will vary.

rose: nose, throws, goes, blows, hose, sews, pose, doze — ___ words

nail: pail, frail, jail, bail, rail, mail, hail, tail — ___ words

bee: see, tea, me, flea, spree, Dee, sea, fee, wee — ___ words

dog: hog, fog, bog, tog, log, frog, jog — ___ words

Rainy Day Riddles

Context Clues

Read the riddle in each puddle. Write the answer on the line.

The things I weave you cannot wear. You could not use my thread to sew on a button. I am a **spider**

I am like a white sheep grazing in a blue field. When the wind comes, I move away fast. I am a **cloud**

The more you use me the smaller I get. One end rubs off what my other end makes. I am a **pencil**

Put me in and out through round holes. Then tie a bow and away we'll go. I am a **shoelace**

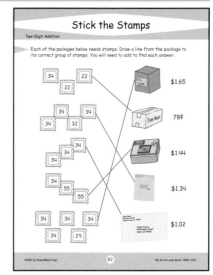

Stick the Stamps

Two-Digit Addition

Each of the packages below needs stamps. Draw a line from the package to its correct group of stamps. You will need to add to find each answer.

$1.65   78¢ $1.44 $1.34 $1.02

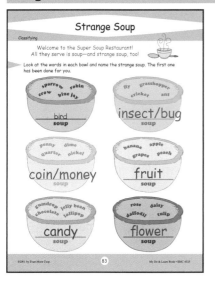

Strange Soup

Classifying

Welcome to the Super Soup Restaurant! All they serve is soup—and strange soup, too!

Look at the words in each bowl and name the strange soup. The first one has been done for you.

sparrow, robin, crow, blue jay — **bird** soup

fly, grasshopper, cricket, ant — **insect/bug** soup

penny, dime, quarter, nickel — **coin/money** soup

banana, apple, grapes, peach — **fruit** soup

gumdrop, jelly bean, chocolate, lollipop — **candy** soup

rose, daisy, daffodil, tulip — **flower** soup

Sally's Spill

Synonyms

Sally Synonym dropped all her words down the stairs. Write the word that means the same as the word on each step. Use the Word Box below.

small — little
funny — silly
unhappy — sad
pretty — lovely
start — begin
tale — story
blossom — flower
bunny — rabbit
icy — cold
child — kid

WORD BOX: cold, flower, lovely, silly, begin, kid, sad, rabbit, story, little

Now write each of the starred (*) letters in order on the lines below to solve this riddle.

What do you call someone whose watch is broken? **late**

Busy, Busy Garden

Fractions

Fill in the blanks. Complete the fraction in each box. There are 8 insects in all.

How many are butterflies? **3**
The butterflies are **3** of the 8 bugs in the garden. 3/8

How many are ladybugs? **2**
The ladybugs are **2** of the 8 bugs in the garden. 2/8

How many are dragonflies? **1**
The dragonfly is **1** of the 8 bugs in the garden. 1/8

How many are bees? **2**
The bees are **2** of the 8 bugs in the garden. 2/8

There is the same fraction of **ladybugs** as **bees** in the garden.

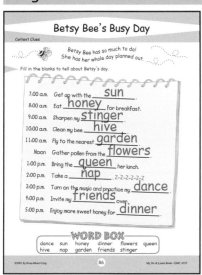

Betsy Bee's Busy Day

Context Clues

Betsy Bee has so much to do! She has her whole day planned out.

Fill in the blanks to tell about Betsy's day.

7:00 a.m. Get up with the **sun**
8:00 a.m. Eat **honey** for breakfast.
9:00 a.m. Sharpen my **stinger**
10:00 a.m. Clean my bee **hive**
11:00 a.m. Fly to the nearest **garden**
Noon Gather pollen from the **flowers**
1:00 p.m. Bring the **queen** her lunch.
2:00 p.m. Take a **nap** z-z-z-z-z-z
3:00 p.m. Turn on the music and practice my **dance**
4:00 p.m. Invite my **friends** over.
5:00 p.m. Enjoy more sweet honey for **dinner**

WORD BOX: dance, sun, honey, flowers, queen, hive, nap, garden, friends, stinger

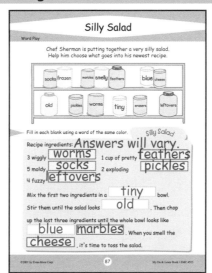

Silly Salad

Word Play

Chef Sherman is putting together a very silly salad. Help him choose what goes into his newest recipe.

socks, frozen, marbles, smelly, feathers, blue, cheese
old, pickles, worms, tiny, erasers, leftovers

Fill in each blank using a word of the same color.

Silly Salad

Recipe ingredients: Answers will vary.
3 wiggly **worms** 1 cup of pretty **feathers**
5 moldy **socks** 2 exploding **pickles**
4 fuzzy **leftovers**

Mix the first two ingredients in a **tiny** bowl.
Stir them until the salad looks **old** . Then chop up the last three ingredients until the whole bowl looks like **blue marbles** . When you smell the **cheese** , it's time to toss the salad.

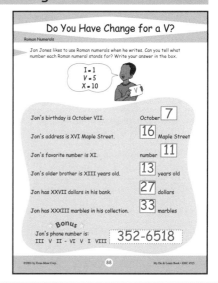

Do You Have Change for a V?

Roman Numerals

Jon Jones likes to use Roman numerals when he writes. Can you tell what number each Roman numeral stands for? Write your answer in the box.

I = 1
V = 5
X = 10

Jon's birthday is October VII. October **7**
Jon's address is XVI Maple Street. **16** Maple Street
Jon's favorite number is XI. number **11**
Jon's older brother is XIII years old. **13** years old
Jon has XXVII dollars in his bank. **27** dollars
Jon has XXXIII marbles in his collection. **33** marbles

Bonus
Jon's phone number is: III V II - VI V I VIII **352-6518**

String Thing
/str/ Blend

Follow the kitty's string and fill in all of the str- words from knot to knot.

not bent — straight
thin piece of leather — strap
road — street
zebras wear them — stripes
small river — stream
not weak — strong
tube used for drinking — straw
a small red fruit — strawberry
weird or unusual — strange
and you're out — strikes

WORD BOX
| straw | strange | stream | strikes | straight |
| strawberry | street | strong | strap | stripes |

©2001 by Evan-Moor Corp. 89 My Do & Learn Book • EMC 4525

Through the Trees
/tr/, /thr/ Blends

We are going for a walk through the woods. As we walk along, we will see lots of things that begin with tr- and thr-.

Use words from the Word Box to fill in the crossword puzzle.

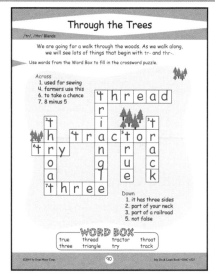

Across
1. used for sewing
4. farmers use this
6. to take a chance
7. 8 minus 5

Down
1. it has three sides
2. part of your neck
3. part of a railroad
5. not false

WORD BOX
| true | thread | tractor | throat |
| three | triangle | try | track |

©2001 by Evan-Moor Corp. 90 My Do & Learn Book • EMC 4525

Aunt Betsy's Bakery
Subtraction

Aunt Betsy has the best bakery! At the end of the day, she has to count the baked goods below to see what is left. Can you help her?

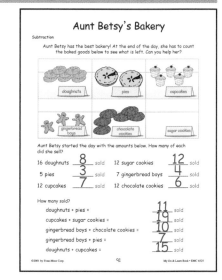

Aunt Betsy started the day with the amounts below. How many of each did she sell?

16 doughnuts — 8 sold   12 sugar cookies — 12 sold
5 pies — 3 sold   7 gingerbread boys — 4 sold
12 cupcakes — 7 sold   12 chocolate cookies — 6 sold

How many sold?
doughnuts + pies = 11 sold
cupcakes + sugar cookies = 19 sold
gingerbread boys + chocolate cookies = 10 sold
gingerbread boys + pies = 7 sold
doughnuts + cupcakes = 15 sold

©2001 by Evan-Moor Corp. 91 My Do & Learn Book • EMC 4525

Join the Club
Classifying

The students at Midtown School want to start some clubs. But they need help naming them.

Match each name choice to the club it would fit. Circle the name you would choose for each club.

Name
Comets
Decimals
Slam Dunks
Wild Cats
Scissors-n-Thread
Galaxies
Home Runs
Bear Buddies
Fractions
Needles and Pins

Club
Sports Club
Math Club
Animal Lovers' Club
Sewing Club
Space Club

©2001 by Evan-Moor Corp. 92 My Do & Learn Book • EMC 4525

Dear Diary
Journaling

Pretend this is a page in your diary. Write about a good day you have had.

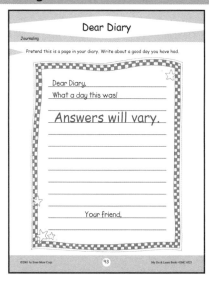

Dear Diary,
What a day this was!

Answers will vary.

Your friend,

©2001 by Evan-Moor Corp. 93 My Do & Learn Book • EMC 4525

Words Worth
Addition

Add to find out what each word is worth. The first one has been done for you.

a = 1¢	e = 5¢	i = 9¢	m = 13¢	q = 17¢	u = 21¢	y = 25¢
b = 2¢	f = 6¢	j = 10¢	n = 14¢	r = 18¢	v = 22¢	z = 26¢
c = 3¢	g = 7¢	k = 11¢	o = 15¢	s = 19¢	w = 23¢	
d = 4¢	h = 8¢	l = 12¢	p = 16¢	t = 20¢	x = 24¢	

fun 6¢ + 21¢ + 14¢ = 41¢   sat 19 . 1 . 20 . 40¢
eat 5 . 1 . 20 . 26¢   mop 13 . 15 . 16 . 44¢
boy 2 . 15 . 25 . 42¢   web 23 . 5 . 2 . 30¢
red 18 . 5 . 4 . 27¢   lip 12 . 9 . 16 . 37¢

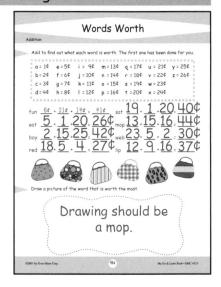

Draw a picture of the word that is worth the most.

Drawing should be a mop.

©2001 by Evan-Moor Corp. 94 My Do & Learn Book • EMC 4525

What Was That?
Punctuation

The punctuation marks are missing from this story. Put them back.

. , ? !

Fred Frog lived in a big pond. He liked to croak, swim, and eat flies all day long. One day a loud sound woke Fred from a nap. Splash! Fred jumped. Where did that sound come from? Splash! Splash! Splash! It was getting closer. Fred looked all around. Then he looked on the shore. There it was. Splash! Splash! Was it something scary? No, it was just a small freckle-faced boy skipping rocks in the water. Fred went back to his nap.

©2001 by Evan-Moor Corp. 95 My Do & Learn Book • EMC 4525

How Do They Compare?
Comparisons

Look at each row of three pictures. One of the pictures has the correct word next to it. Add er or est to the other two words.

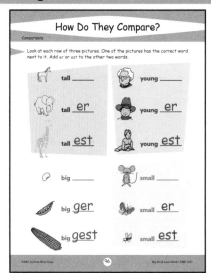

tall ____
tall er
tall est

young ____
young er
young est

big ____
big ger
big gest

small ____
small er
small est

©2001 by Evan-Moor Corp. 96 My Do & Learn Book • EMC 4525

Crazy About Crayons
Greater Than, Less Than, Equal To

Use this graph to compare the number of crayons the children have. Use one of these symbols in each box below.

> more than   < less than   = equal to

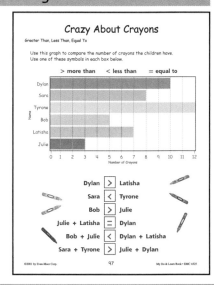

Dylan > Latisha
Sara < Tyrone
Bob > Julie
Julie + Latisha = Dylan
Bob + Julie < Dylan + Latisha
Sara + Tyrone > Julie + Dylan

©2001 by Evan-Moor Corp. 97 My Do & Learn Book • EMC 4525

Page 100

First, Next, and Last

Sequencing

Stories happen in order. First . . . next . . . last!

I got money from my bank.	I went to the ice-cream man.	I bought a cherry Popsicle.
First	**Next**	**Last**

Draw your own story in order. Then tell about each part.

Drawings
and
stories
will vary.

First   **Next**   **Last**

©2001 by Evan-Moor Corp.   98   My Do & Learn Book • EMC 4525

Page 101

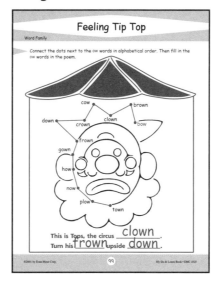

Feeling Tip Top

Word Family

Connect the dots next to the *ow* words in alphabetical order. Then fill in the *ow* words in the poem.

cow   brown   down   crown   clown   bow   frown   gown   how   now   plow   town

This is Tops, the circus **clown**.
Turn his **frown** upside **down**.

©2001 by Evan-Moor Corp.   99   My Do & Learn Book • EMC 4525

Page 102

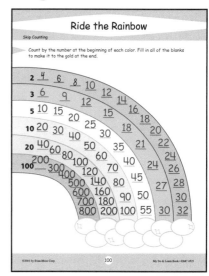

Ride the Rainbow

Skip Counting

Count by the number at the beginning of each color. Fill in all of the blanks to make it to the gold at the end.

2 4 6 8 10 ...
3 6 9 12 ...
5 10 15 20 ...
10 20 30 40 ...
20 40 60 80 ...
100 200 300 400 ...

©2001 by Evan-Moor Corp.   100   My Do & Learn Book • EMC 4525

Page 103

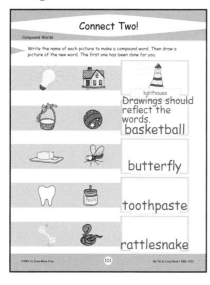

Connect Two!

Compound Words

Write the name of each picture to make a compound word. Then draw a picture of the new word. The first one has been done for you.

lighthouse

Drawings should reflect the words.

basketball

butterfly

toothpaste

rattlesnake

©2001 by Evan-Moor Corp.   101   My Do & Learn Book • EMC 4525

Page 104

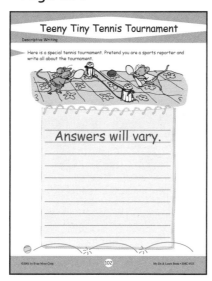

Teeny Tiny Tennis Tournament

Descriptive Writing

Here is a special tennis tournament. Pretend you are a sports reporter and write all about the tournament.

Answers will vary.

©2001 by Evan-Moor Corp.   102   My Do & Learn Book • EMC 4525

Page 105

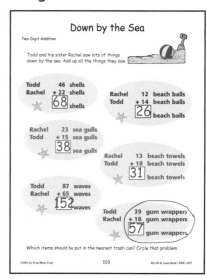

Down by the Sea

Two-Digit Addition

Todd and his sister Rachel saw lots of things down by the sea. Add up all the things they saw.

Todd 46 shells / Rachel + 22 shells = **68** shells

Rachel 12 beach balls / Todd + 14 beach balls = **26** beach balls

Rachel 23 sea gulls / Todd + 15 sea gulls = **38** sea gulls

Rachel 13 beach towels / Todd + 18 beach towels = **31** beach towels

Todd 87 waves / Rachel + 65 waves = **152** waves

Todd 39 gum wrappers / Rachel + 18 gum wrappers = **57** gum wrappers

Which items should be put in the nearest trash can? Circle that problem.

©2001 by Evan-Moor Corp.   103   My Do & Learn Book • EMC 4525

Page 106

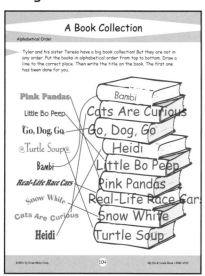

A Book Collection

Alphabetical Order

Tyler and his sister Teresa have a big book collection! But they are not in any order. Put the books in alphabetical order from top to bottom. Draw a line to the correct place. Then write the title on the book. The first one has been done for you.

Pink Pandas, Little Bo Peep, Go, Dog, Go, Turtle Soup, Bambi, Real-Life Race Cars, Snow White, Cats Are Curious, Heidi

Bambi
Cats Are Curious
Go, Dog, Go
Heidi
Little Bo Peep
Pink Pandas
Real-Life Race Cars
Snow White
Turtle Soup

©2001 by Evan-Moor Corp.   104   My Do & Learn Book • EMC 4525

Page 107

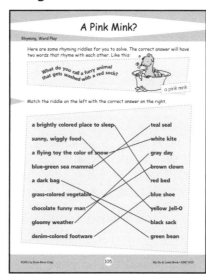

A Pink Mink?

Rhyming, Word Play

Here are some rhyming riddles for you to solve. The correct answer will have two words that rhyme with each other. Like this:

What do you call a furry animal that gets washed with a red sock? — a pink mink

Match the riddle on the left with the correct answer on the right.

a brightly colored place to sleep — teal seal
sunny, wiggly food — white kite
a flying toy the color of snow — gray day
blue-green sea mammal — brown clown
a dark bag — red bed
grass-colored vegetable — blue shoe
chocolate funny man — yellow Jell-O
gloomy weather — black sack
denim-colored footwear — green bean

©2001 by Evan-Moor Corp.   105   My Do & Learn Book • EMC 4525

Page 108

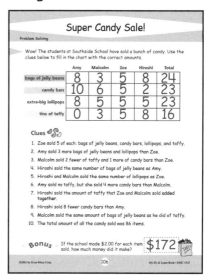

Super Candy Sale!

Problem Solving

Wow! The students at Southside School have sold a bunch of candy. Use the clues below to fill in the chart with the correct amounts.

	Amy	Malcolm	Zoe	Hiroshi	Total
bags of jelly beans	8	3	5	8	24
candy bars	10	6	5	2	23
extra-big lollipops	8	5	5	5	23
tins of taffy	0	3	5	8	16

Clues

1. Zoe sold 5 of each: bags of jelly beans, candy bars, lollipops, and taffy.
2. Amy sold 3 more bags of jelly beans and lollipops than Zoe.
3. Malcolm sold 2 fewer of taffy and 1 more of candy bars than Zoe.
4. Hiroshi and Malcolm sold the same number of lollipops as Zoe.
5. Amy sold no taffy, but she sold 4 more candy bars than Malcolm.
6. Hiroshi sold the same number of bags of jelly beans as Amy.
7. Hiroshi sold the amount of taffy that Zoe and Malcolm sold added together.
8. Hiroshi sold 8 fewer candy bars than Amy.
9. Malcolm sold the same amount of bags of jelly beans as he did of taffy.
10. The total amount of all the candy sold was 86 items.

Bonus If the school made $2.00 for each item sold, how much money did it make? **$172**

©2001 by Evan-Moor Corp.   106   My Do & Learn Book • EMC 4525

Thanks a Bunch!
Spelling

Millie wrote a nice thank-you note to her aunt for her birthday present. The words in red print will give you clues about what the birthday present was. Use the Word Box to help you unscramble the words.

Dear Aunt Clara,
Thank you so much for the amazing present. I was so surprised to see its whiskers poking out of the box. Then I opened it. Your present was furry and alive! It had a long tail and pink eyes. I am so glad you also gave me a cage, wheel, and cheese, too. I like to feed it some seeds and cheese. At first Mom was afraid of it. But once it wiggled its little nose at her, she was fine.
Thanks again for my wonderful little mouse.
Your loving niece,
Millie

WORD BOX
cheese · eyes · nose · furry · amazing · alive
whiskers · cage · tail · seeds · wiggled · wheel

Millie's present was a __mouse__.

Fun with Fill-ins!
Parts of Speech

Choose any word from the same color group to write in each blank. Make a funny or real story. It's up to you!

Nouns (naming words)	Verbs	Adjectives
treasure · cookies		
snowman · river		
cave · doughnuts		
garbage · puddle		
bunnies · cactus		
mountain · skunk		

Note: You may add *-ed* to these words.

What a _____ day this was! First I found some _____ . But I had to across a _____ to get to them. Then I had to _____ through a _____ filled with _____ . They made me feel _____ .
When that was done, I _____ with a rope across a _____ , I could smell some _____ right around the corner. I could hardly wait to _____ them! After going through one more _____ , I was there! At last, I could _____ and _____ some

_____ Answers will vary.

Carly the Coupon Clipper
Two-Digit Subtraction

Carly loves to clip coupons and save money by using them. Draw a line from the coupon to the product. Carly did not use one of her coupons. The first one has been done for you.

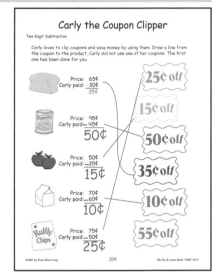

Price: 65¢
Carly paid: −30¢
35¢ — 25¢ off

Price: 95¢
Carly paid: −45¢
50¢ — 15¢ off

Price: 50¢
Carly paid: −35¢
15¢ — 50¢ off

Price: 70¢
Carly paid: −60¢
10¢ — 35¢ off

Price: 75¢
Carly paid: −50¢
25¢ — 10¢ off

55¢ off

Prefix Pyramids
Prefixes

Artie the Archaeologist needs your help to rebuild some pyramids. Fill in each pyramid using words that begin with the prefix at the top. Use the words in the Word Box to help you build the words.

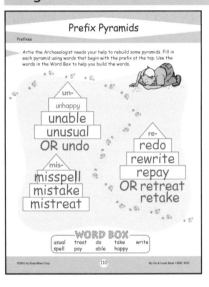

un-
unhappy
unable
unusual
OR undo

re-
redo
rewrite
repay
OR retreat
retake

mis-
misspell
mistake
mistreat

WORD BOX
usual · treat · do · take · write
spell · pay · able · happy

What Am I?
Syllables

Count the syllables. Color.

1-syllable words green
2-syllable words blue
3-syllable words red
4-syllable words yellow

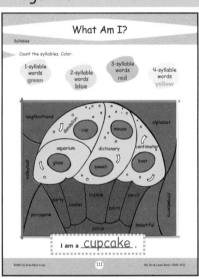

I am a __cupcake__.

Sum Time
Addition Facts

Fill in the blocks with a number that will make each row across add up to 12. Then add down and write the sum of each column in the box.

3	1	8	12
5	7	0	12
4	6	2	12
12	14	10	

In the Sea
Visual Discrimination

There are so many things in the sea. But sometimes they are hard to find. Find and circle all the words in the Word Box.

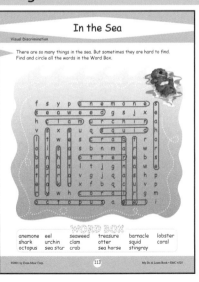

WORD BOX
anemone · eel · seaweed · treasure · barnacle · lobster
shark · urchin · clam · otter · sea horse · coral
octopus · sea star · crab · squid · stingray

The Birthday Bash
Vocabulary

This crossword puzzle is filled with birthday party words. Fill it in. Then unscramble the letters in the yellow squares to answer the riddle below.

Down
1. it's the main dish
3. it comes once a year
5. you play these, like Pin the Tail on the Donkey
6. it says "Happy Birthday!" and is hung up
7. he wears a big red nose

Across
2. you blow these out
4. you win this
5. the people at your party
8. you blow these up
9. you open these

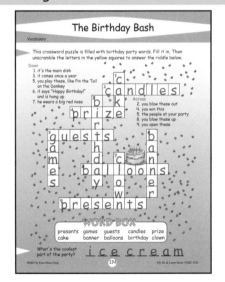

candles
prize
guests
balloons
presents

WORD BOX
presents · games · guests · candles · prize
cake · banner · balloons · birthday · clown

What's the coolest part of the party? __ice cream__

Gumball Game
Two-Digit Addition

Find the gumball needed to complete each problem.

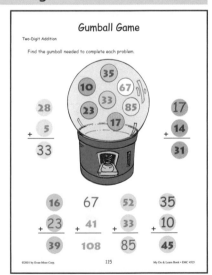

28
+ 5
33

17
+ 14
31

16
+ 23
39

67
+ 41
108

52
+ 33
85

35
+ 10
45

Page 118

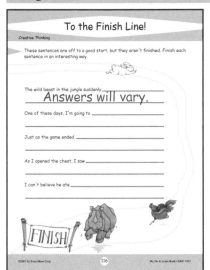

To the Finish Line!

Creative Thinking

These sentences are off to a good start, but they aren't finished. Finish each sentence in an interesting way.

The wild beast in the jungle suddenly
<u>Answers will vary.</u>

One of these days, I'm going to _____

Just as the game ended, _____

As I opened the chest, I saw _____

I can't believe he ate _____

Page 119

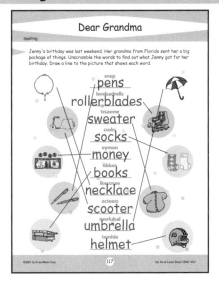

Dear Grandma

Spelling

Jenny's birthday was last weekend. Her grandma from Florida sent her a big package of things. Unscramble the words to find out what Jenny got for her birthday. Draw a line to the picture that shows each word.

snep — pens
lorebadrells — rollerblades
trsaeew — sweater
csoks — socks
eymon — money
obkos — books
lkecrene — necklace
octoers — scooter
merlabul — umbrella
temhle — helmet

Page 120

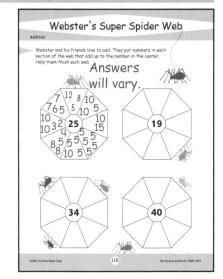

Webster's Super Spider Web

Addition

Webster and his friends love to add. They put numbers in each section of the web that add up to the number in the center. Help them finish each web.

Answers will vary.

25   19

34   40

Page 121

Put an End to It!

Suffixes

Each of the words in the Word Box has an ending, or suffix. Circle each suffix. Then use the words to complete the crossword puzzle.

Across
2. a special feeling between two people
6. not afraid
7. opposite of slowly

Down
1. a pipe cleaner is _____
3. wet weather
4. a machine to clean clothes
5. a kind a hint

friendship
bendable
rainy
fearless
washer
helpful
quickly

quickly   bendable   washer   rainy
friendship   fearless   helpful

Page 122

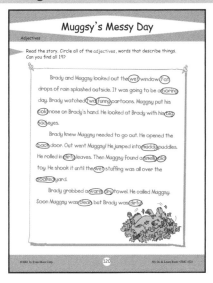

Muggsy's Messy Day

Adjectives

Read the story. Circle all of the adjectives, words that describe things. Can you find all 19?

Brady and Muggsy looked out the wet window. Fat drops of rain splashed outside. It was going to be a boring day. Brady watched two funny cartoons. Muggsy put his cold nose on Brady's hand. He looked at Brady with his big sad eyes.

Brady knew Muggsy needed to go out. He opened the back door. Out went Muggsy! He jumped into muddy puddles. He rolled in dirty leaves. Then Muggsy found a smelly old toy. He shook it until the wet stuffing was all over the soaked yard.

Brady grabbed a warm dry towel. He called Muggsy. Soon Muggsy was clean but Brady was dirty.

Page 123

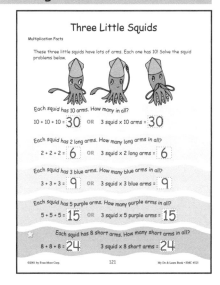

Three Little Squids

Multiplication Facts

These three little squids have lots of arms. Each one has 10! Solve the squid problems below.

Each squid has 10 arms. How many in all?
10 + 10 + 10 = 30   OR   3 squid x 10 arms = 30

Each squid has 2 long arms. How many long arms in all?
2 + 2 + 2 = 6   OR   3 squid x 2 long arms = 6

Each squid has 3 blue arms. How many blue arms in all?
3 + 3 + 3 = 9   OR   3 squid x 3 blue arms = 9

Each squid has 5 purple arms. How many purple arms in all?
5 + 5 + 5 = 15   OR   3 squid x 5 purple arms = 15

Each squid has 8 short arms. How many short arms in all?
8 + 8 + 8 = 24   OR   3 squid x 8 short arms = 24

Page 124

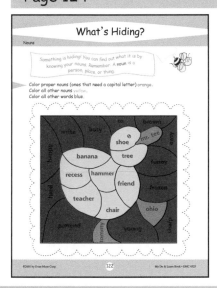

What's Hiding?

Nouns

Something is hiding! You can find out what it is by knowing your nouns. Remember: A noun is a person, place, or thing.

Color proper nouns (ones that need a capital letter) orange.
Color all other nouns yellow.
Color all other words blue.

Page 125

What Makes a Perfect Pet?

Narrative Writing

Tell what a perfect pet is like.

<u>Answers will vary.</u>

Now write a newspaper ad. Be sure to say what this pet will be like and include your name and phone number.

Wanted: A Perfect Pet

Page 126

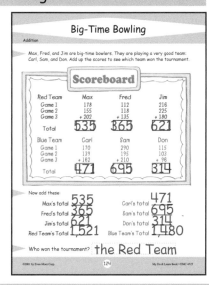

Big-Time Bowling

Addition

Max, Fred, and Jim are big-time bowlers. They are playing a very good team: Carl, Sam, and Don. Add up the scores to see which team won the tournament.

Scoreboard

Red Team	Max	Fred	Jim
Game 1	178	112	216
Game 2	155	118	225
Game 3	+ 202	+ 135	+ 180
Total	535	865	621

Blue Team	Carl	Sam	Don
Game 1	170	290	115
Game 2	139	195	103
Game 3	+ 162	+ 210	+ 96
Total	471	695	314

Now add these:
Max's total 535
Fred's total 365
Jim's total 621
Red Team's Total 1,521

Carl's total 471
Sam's total 695
Don's total 314
Blue Team's Total 1,480

Who won the tournament? **the Red Team**

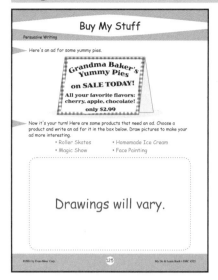

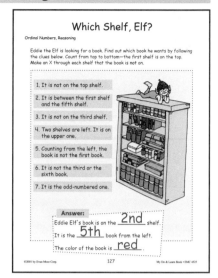